# Larry Bird: The Inspiring Story of One of Basketball's Greatest Forwards

An Unauthorized Biography

By: Clayton Geoffreys

Copyright © 2016 by Calvintir Books, LLC

All rights reserved. Neither this book nor any portion thereof may be reproduced or used in any manner whatsoever without the express written permission. Published in the United States of America.

**Disclaimer**: The following book is for entertainment and informational purposes only. The information presented is without contract or any type of guarantee assurance. While every caution has been taken to provide accurate and current information, it is solely the reader's responsibility to check all information contained in this article before relying upon it. Neither the author nor publisher can be held accountable for any errors or omissions.

Under no circumstances will any legal responsibility or blame be held against the author or publisher for any reparation, damages, or monetary loss due to the information presented, either directly or indirectly. This book is not intended as legal or medical advice. If any such specialized advice is needed, seek a qualified individual for help.

Trademarks are used without permission. Use of the trademark is not authorized by, associated with, or sponsored by the trademark owners. All trademarks and brands used within this book are used with no intent to infringe on the trademark owners and only used for clarifying purposes.

This book is not sponsored by or affiliated with the National Basketball Association, its teams, the players, or anyone involved with them.

Visit my website at www.claytongeoffreys.com
Cover photo by Kurt Shimala is licensed under CC BY 2.0 / modified from original

# Table of Contents

Foreword ........................................................................... 1

Introduction ....................................................................... 2

Chapter 1: Childhood and Early Life ................................ 6

Chapter 2: High School Career ......................................... 8

Chapter 3: College Career ............................................... 11

Chapter 4: Larry Bird's NBA Career ............................... 15

    Getting Drafted ........................................................... 15

    Rookie Season ............................................................. 18

    The Dawn of the Boston Big Three, First NBA Title .... 22

    Falling Short ............................................................... 29

    First MVP, Finals Battle with the Lakers, Second NBA Title ............................................................................. 36

    Second MVP, Finals Rematch with the Lakers ............ 44

    MVP Three-Peat, Third NBA Championship .............. 52

    50-40-90 Season, Last Finals Appearance ................... 61

Second 50-40-90 Season, End of the Reign as the Kings of the East .................................................. 70

Injury Season ........................................................... 75

Return from Injury, First Round Exit ........................... 76

Injury-Prone Season, Beginning of the End of a Legendary Career .................................................... 78

Final NBA Season ...................................................... 81

1992 Olympics: The Dream Team ................................. 83

Chapter 5: Life After Retirement ............................................ 85

Boston's Special Assistant .......................................... 85

Coaching the Indiana Pacers ...................................... 85

Executive Stint ......................................................... 91

Chapter 6: Rivalry with Magic Johnson ................................... 93

Chapter 7: Larry Bird's Personal Life ..................................... 100

Chapter 8: Larry Bird's Impact on Basketball ........................ 102

Chapter 9: Larry Bird's Legacy ............................................ 106

Final Word/About the Author .............................................. 112

References ........................................................................ 115

# Foreword

Larry Bird is easily considered one of the greatest players of all time to grace the hardwood. A three-time NBA Champion, Larry Bird led the Celtics throughout the 1980s as well as the league, exemplifying a high degree of excellence on both ends of the floor. He led the Celtics in their re-emergence as a franchise and became one of the staple individuals forever associated to the organization, much like how Michael Jordan is to the Chicago Bulls. Larry Bird continues his involvement with the game of basketball as the president of basketball operations for the Indiana Pacers, where he previously coached from 1997 to 2000. Thank you for purchasing *Larry Bird: The Inspiring Story of One of Basketball's Greatest Forwards*. In this unauthorized biography, we will learn Larry Bird's incredible life story and impact on the game of basketball. Hope you enjoy and if you do, please do not forget to leave a review!

Also, check out my website at claytongeoffreys.com to join my exclusive list where I let you know about my latest books. To thank you for your purchase, you can go to my site to download a free copy of *33 Life Lessons: Success Principles, Career Advice & Habits of Successful People*. In the book, you'll learn from some of the greatest thought leaders of different industries on what it takes to become successful and how to live a great life.

Cheers,

*Clayton Geoffreys*

*Visit me at www.claytongeoffreys.com*

# Introduction

If there were a player in the history of the NBA that deserves to be called a legend, that man would be none other than Larry Bird. All-Star appearances, clutch plays, highlight moments, personal awards, MVP's, and championships. You can name any accolade in the NBA, and Larry Bird has achieved them all in his truly stellar 13-year NBA career. Just looking at all those achievements and his career averages of 24.3 points, ten rebounds, 6.3 assists, and 1.7 steals, you would immediately understand why he is a legitimate NBA legend.

Larry Bird is also considered as one of the best shooters in the history of the league. In Bird, you have a guy standing almost 6'10" who could shoot the lights out of the basketball. He has the size of a power forward but with the shooting touch of an off guard. No wonder he has a career shooting percentage of 49.6% from the floor, 37.6% from the three-point line, and 88.6% from the foul stripe. With those shooting numbers, Larry Bird was a two-time member of the 50-40-90 club. Though Larry's offensive skill set belonged to that of a shooting guard, he could pass the ball as well as a point guard while rebounding possessions at the rate of a center. With those skills and abilities,

Larry Bird is also one of the most versatile players the NBA has ever seen.

Achievements, statistics, and skills aside, what made Larry Bird one of the most iconic legends the NBA has ever seen was how he made the NBA relevant again. During the 70's, the league saw a decline in viewership and popularity. While there were still transcendent superstars in that era of basketball, no team dominated the NBA landscape, and no player captured the imagination of fans while also bringing in success during the playoffs. There were eight different champions in that decade, but none of the players that those championship teams had were so famous or awe-inspiring that they made the NBA the most relevant professional league in the world.[i] The NBA struggled to get lucrative television contracts while also finding stadiums far under full capacity. It was also during that decade that African-American rights movements were at their peak and white people refused to watch a basketball league dominated by "selfish" black players.[ii]

It was Larry Bird, along with his rival Magic Johnson, who made the NBA popular again when he came into the league in the final season of the 70's decade. Bird came into the NBA as a perennial winner in the collegiate rankings. As a white man, he was doing things black players could not do while also leading a team dominated by fellow white men. Bird immediately dominated the NBA despite lacking the strength and athletic abilities of his black counterparts. He not only got fellow white men interested in the NBA again, he also got the league the popularity it deserved thanks to one of the most exciting rivalries the world has ever seen.

In 1979, Larry Bird was drafted by the Boston Celtics, the winningest franchise in the NBA at the time. Bird led a Celtic revolution that made the team one of the most dominant squads in the NBA during that decade. On the flipside, the Los Angeles Lakers, in the same year, drafted a 6'9" player with point guard skills. That man was Earvin Johnson, who would later become better known as "Magic." Magic revived a Lakers franchise into a high-octane running team that got fans excited every single second.

With Bird leading a dominant Celtics squad and with Magic running the most exciting offense in the NBA that decade, it was inevitable that the two best players would meet in classic clashes for league supremacy. Matchups between the Celtics and the Lakers often turned into some of the best games in the history of the NBA. The rivalry between the two storied franchises trickled down into a rivalry between Larry Bird and Magic Johnson, both of whom coincidentally also had a mini-rivalry against each other back in their college days. The heated rivalry between Larry and Magic headlined the NBA's resurgence in the 80's decade. In essence, Bird and Johnson had a big hand in saving the NBA.

While it is hard not to mention Magic Johnson's name when talking about Larry Bird, the legendary Celtic leader was a player of such a caliber that he would have stood out even if his eternal rival had never existed. Bird, in the biggest stages and the most important games, often delivered and gave the Celtics wins and championships. Whenever opposing stars would come out to play big, Larry made sure he played bigger. Whenever opposing teams were hungry to win games or titles, Bird made sure his team was hungrier. As good a player and winner as he was, Bird's competitive edge, transcendent skills, and popularity are all just a few reasons why he is considered the NBA's consummate legend.

# Chapter 1: Childhood and Early Life

Larry Bird's legendary career and superstar status had humble beginnings in the small town of West Baden, Indiana. Larry was born on December 7, 1956, back when West Baden was a town of barely a couple of thousand people. He was the fourth child of a married couple named Joe and Georgia Bird. In later years, the Bird household moved to the nearby city of French Lick, which was just slightly bigger than West Baden, but more popular because of the town's springs, which were tourist destinations. The family made the move because Joe found work in one of French Lick's factories.[iii]

Because of the simple job that Joe, the family's patriarch, had been working on for years, the Bird family lived a humble life. However, the size of the household and the falling fortunes of the town had the Bird family often struggling to fulfill their needs. They were living paycheck to paycheck through Joe Bird's job in the factories. They would often even have to fight to resist the freezing temperatures at night when the home's furnace broke down.[iii] That humble and hard life molded the young Larry Bird into the blue-collar basketball player and consummate worker he always was in the NBA.

To escape the harsh realities of living off their father's meager earnings, the Bird brothers passed the time by playing outdoor sports such as basketball, softball, and baseball. Even at a young age, Larry Bird was already a sports enthusiast that loved to compete as much as he could. Larry was so fond of all sorts of outdoor sports that he did not dedicate his efforts into honing his skills and talents in just one of them. It was only when he entered Springs Valley High School that he finally settled with basketball, the sport in which he became a legend.[iii]

# Chapter 2: High School Career

Larry Bird entered Springs Valley High School as a member of their varsity basketball team. While Bird was fond of playing various sports in his younger years, he decided to dedicate his full effort into playing basketball because he realized that he had a chance of making himself an excellent player in that game. Ever the hard blue-collar worker, Larry Bird poured all of his enthusiasm and efforts into developing his skills as a basketball player. He would practice by himself or with his teammates day and night despite the harsh cold weather and the many pains he was feeling physically. It was the family's humble life that kept Larry working so hard. It was what motivated him into trying his best to work out of his harsh beginnings.[iii]

Larry Bird started playing as a guard for Springs Valley in the early parts of his high school career. He had the right size of for shooting guard at that age at 6'3". He practiced day and night to develop the skills needed for a shooting guard. No wonder he was such a great shooter when he came into the NBA even at his height and size.

Larry continued to play the off guard position up until his junior year in high school. His junior year was a resurgent one for him because he had just come back from an ankle injury that kept him out for most of the season in his sophomore year. It was in his junior year when his star started to shine. Bird was a focal point to Springs Valley's incredible 19-2 season that year. He was so popular among the local folks that the love trickled down to his family, who would often get free rides from neighbors, who knew that the Bird household could not afford to buy their own car.[iv]

Though Larry wanted more than anything just to focus on honing his skills and talents in the game of basketball, things back at home were not all that simple for a growing and maturing teenager. His parents Joe and Georgia divorced sometime in Larry's senior year. The divorce had the Bird household struggling more than they ever had. Larry, in turn, would not let the troubles faze him, focusing more than ever in basketball as a means of escaping his reality.

It was a good thing that Bird's genetics were coping with his desires to play basketball at a high level. The former 6'3" shooting guard saw a growth spurt in his senior year. In his final year in high school, Larry Bird grew to about 6'7". With the increase in his height, Bird moved over to the forward spot and became the best player that Springs Valley High School has ever produced. Larry Bird averaged an incredible stat line of 31 points and 21 rebounds while mixing up the skills he developed as a shooting guard together with his newfound role as a big-time rebounder inside the paint.

Larry Bird was so good in his senior year that he was the main attraction of what was an otherwise small town. Though French Lick had a population of just a little over 2,000 people, many people from the surrounding cities and towns would come and visit just to see Larry Bird strut his stuff on the hardwood floor. Bird was so popular within the county that the attendance to his games would sometimes reach as much as 1,600 people. In his final high school game, the beloved Larry Bird was cheered on by as many as 4,000 fans.[iv]

# Chapter 3: College Career

Larry Bird's legendary exploits in high school and his popularity at the prep level earned him a scholarship to Indiana University to play for legendary head coach Bob Knight in 1974. Though Bird was always a hard-working basketball player, he was uncomfortable in college. He was so used to living a rural lifestyle in a small town that he felt that he was not at home on the large campus of Indiana University. For a long time, critics thought that Bird had left because he did not get along with Bobby Knight. But he would clarify that issue by saying that he simply was not used to the large university campus.[vi] Larry would only last 24 days as an Indiana University Hoosier before deciding to drop out and return to French Lick.

Upon his return to his hometown, Larry Bird immediately enrolled at a community college called Northwood Institute. Bird lasted a year in Northwood Institute. At that time, Larry Bird was a married man and had a daughter named Corrie. He would file for divorce soon after in what appeared to be a short-lived marriage. Larry would take up a municipal job at the French Lick City Department to make ends meet and to support his daughter. His primary job was as a garbage truck driver, but would sometimes help with the maintenance of the town's roads.

Though the job seemed simple, Bird enjoyed doing it because it kept him sociable with the townsfolk and gave him the chance to help make the community a better place.

Though Bird enjoyed a simple and easy life at that span of his career, tragedy struck. He would find out that Joe Bird, his father, had committed suicide. To escape the grief and the sadness that came with his father's death, Larry would turn to basketball again. In 1975, he would enroll at Indiana State University. The Indiana State Sycamores were not a very successful basketball squad, only having won 24 of their last 52 games. Unfortunately for them, Larry Bird could not bring them out of limbo in the 1975-76 season as the Springs Valley product had to sit out due to NCAA eligibility issues.

When Larry Bird joined the team in the 1976-77 season, he singlehandedly turned the Sycamore's fortunes around. He was leading the team in almost every statistical category while giving Indiana State more victories than they had ever experienced in the past in just his first season. Like he used to do in Springs Valley, Larry was packing the house full with more than 3,000 fans cheering for him. The sharpshooting 6'9" forward was the attraction that made Indiana State a popular team. The Sycamores were 25-3 in Bird's first season. He averaged 32.8 points, 13.3 rebounds, and 4.4 assists while shooting 54.4% from the floor.

Larry Bird would come back just as strong in his second season with the Indiana Sycamores. He led the team once again in almost every statistical category while also winning at the same rate he had in the past season. He averaged 30 points, 11.5 rebounds, and 3.9 assists, and was named the Conference Player of the Year that season. After his second season and junior year in college, Larry Bird was a finished product ready to storm into the NBA. A team had already chosen him in the 1978 NBA Draft. Ever the hard worker and knowing that he only had one chance to earn a college degree, Larry Bird decided to play for one more year with Indiana State.[iii]

With Larry Bird leading the way with normal numbers of 28.6 points, 14.9 rebounds, and 5.5 assists, the Sycamores were unbeatable and they opened the season with no losses. Bird was named the Naismith College Player of the Year in his final season in college. The Sycamores were just as unbeatable in the NCAA tournament. The Indiana State Sycamores would reach the NCAA Championship game against the Michigan State Spartans.[iv] It was during the NCAA Championship that one of the greatest rivalries in sports history blossomed.

Larry Bird's Sycamores faced a Spartans team led by Magic Johnson, a 6'9" point guard with fantastic passing abilities and all-around skills. That was the first time the two transcendent talents and future NBA legends faced each other in a basketball game. Unfortunately, Bird was not in his full form that game. He struggled to score 19 points on 7 out of 21 shooting from the field. The Michigan State Spartans would defeat Larry's Sycamores in that championship game. Nevertheless, Larry Bird enjoyed a very successful career in Indiana State while also earning a college degree. He was on his way to the NBA after that loss to the Spartans.

# Chapter 4: Larry Bird's NBA Career

## Getting Drafted

Larry Bird had already applied for the NBA Draft back in 1978 just after his junior year in college and his second playing season with the Indiana State Sycamores. Larry spent about two years without playing competitive basketball because he went to a local community college after dropping out of Indiana University in 1975. Because he was not eligible in his freshman year with the Sycamores, it did not seem like he missed a beat or even lost his shooting touch when he suited up for Indiana State in the 1976-77 and the 1977-78 seasons. He averaged over 30 points and over ten rebounds in each of those two years.

Unlike a lot of NBA prospects, Bird did not achieve enormous numbers in college because he was a dominant force on the hard floor. Larry was playing in a sport dominated by bigger, stronger, and more athletic black men. He was just a tall white guy with no other outstanding physical attributes. Bird did not jump out at the gym, could not run like a gazelle, and could not outmuscle his defenders. For all his physical limitations, Larry Bird was the hardest worker on the court. He was the most competitive out of his teammates. And he was the hungriest out of the bunch. Whatever he lacked physically, he more than made up by working harder on his game and by competing better than every other guy.

His work ethic and hunger to get better led Larry Bird to develop skills unheard of from a man standing nearly 6'10". In the collegiate ranks and even back in his prep years, Larry had already developed a shooting touch that could trump shooting guards. You take a man standing more than 6'9" and give him the range and accuracy of an off guard, and what you get is an un-guardable shooter from the perimeter.

As good of a shooter that Bird was, he was not a one-trick pony. He knew how to use his height and length to score above smaller defenders inside the paint. Larry had an uncanny finesse when finishing baskets amongst the tall trees because he lacked the athleticism to simply out-jump the shot blockers. Bird, for all his athletic shortcomings, was, interestingly, also fond of running the fast break either by running the floor without the ball or by initiating it himself.[v]

Scoring was not the only thing that Larry Bird could do, he was also a superb passer. He could find open men when he had the ball at the top of the key, or he could make plays from the high post. It helped that his height and length made it easier for him to hit open men. When initiating the break, Bird was also a willing passer to streaking teammates. Larry, despite being comparatively vertically grounded, could rebound the ball at a very high rate. He knew how to follow up his misses and could block out opponents to get good positions for rebounds.

Defensively, Larry Bird was never a slacker. He did not have the foot speed to follow quicker and faster players. However, Bird was always a talented position defender. He would try his best to beat his opponents to the position instead of just trying to keep up with their speed. With his length, he could cover shots or get his hands through passing lanes for steals.

For all of his amazing abilities and skills on the basketball court, one would consider Larry Bird to be one of the top, if not the top, prospects in the 1978 NBA Draft. However, Bird fell a few spots below the coveted top overall draft pick. Before joining the draft, Larry had already decided that he would finish his four years in college. The Indiana Pacers had formerly owned the top pick in the 1978 draft, and they were intent on taking Larry Bird with that pick. However, they failed to convince the Indiana State forward to forego his final year of college. Fearing that Bird might sign with another team in 1979 even if they drafted him in 1978, they traded the pick over to the Portland Trailblazers, who also failed to convince Larry to go straight to the NBA.[vi]

Instead of becoming the top overall pick, Larry Bird got passed on by five teams, who all might have feared they would lose the versatile forward to another team when he finally decided to join the NBA in 1979. Gambling on their chances, the Boston Celtics, the franchise with the most NBA titles, chose Bird with the sixth overall pick in the 1978 NBA Draft. As planned, Larry went on to finish his final year with the Sycamores. After a runner-up finish to Magic Johnson's Spartans in the 1979 NCAA Tournament, Bird signed a $3.25 million five-year contract with the Celtics. Larry, at that time, was the highest-paid rookie in the history of any professional sport. Despite the lucrative contract he earned, Bird would never forget his humble beginnings as a blue collar athlete from a small town in Indiana.[iii]

## Rookie Season

Larry Bird was set to join a Boston Celtics team that, historically, has been one of the best, if not the best, teams the NBA could ever offer to the world. However, the Celtics, entering the 1979-80 season, were in a mini-slump after winning the NBA title in 1976. They only won 29 of their 82 games during the 1978-79 season, and they were only 32-50 in 1977-78 as they struggled to get wins in the post-Havlicek era.

The arrival of Larry brought a lot of optimism to the Boston fan base.

But Bird was not going to right the Boston ship all by himself that season. He was coming in with a lot of help. Former scoring champion point guard Tiny Archibald was there to run the offense and make plays for Larry. The rising forward Cedric Maxwell provided a lot of scoring at the wing. Of course, he had veteran All-Star big man Dave Cowens teaching him the ins and outs of professional life and the culture of being a Celtic. Bird even played with the great Pete Maravich in the latter's heydays that season.

With the right pieces surrounding him and with a lot of optimism and support from the fan base despite criticisms from detractors that said he was too slow for the NBA[vi], Larry Bird emerged as a rookie star. In his first game as a rookie, he had 14 points when the Celtics defeated the Houston Rockets. He had his breakout game in only his second outing, scoring 28 points in a game against the Cleveland Cavaliers. Bird would lead Boston to a 4-0 start and to 10-2 throughout their first 12 games.

On December 28, 1979, Larry Bird would face Magic Johnson and the Los Angeles Lakers for the first time since the latter beat him in the 1979 NCAA Finals. It was the first game of what was to become the best one-on-one rivalry in the history of the NBA and even possibly the annals of professional sports. In that game, Larry would score 16 points. Despite his efforts, Bird fell short against Magic yet again. The playmaker finished with 23 points to lead the Lakers past the Celtics in the two transcendent rookies' first meeting in the NBA. The two would meet for a second time that season on January 13, 1980, in Boston. On a one-on-one basis, Bird's 14 points trumped Magic, who finished with merely a point. However, the Lakers won that bout yet again.

On January 27, Larry Bird would have his then-best performance as a professional basketballer. He finished with 36 points in a 23-point win against the then-San Diego Clippers. That game was the start of what was to become a seven-game streak for the Boston Celtics. Bird also earned a personal milestone that season when he was selected as a member of the Eastern Conference All-Star squad. Yes, Larry Bird was a rookie All-Star, he was that good. Though the winning streak ended on February 13, Larry tried his best to keep the team rolling when he went for a then-career high of 45 big points.

Larry Bird would go for at least 40 points again when he scored 41 in a win against the Detroit Pistons on March 2. Bird's star would never fall from then on as he led the Boston Celtics to a

17-6 finish through their final 22 games. There was no doubt that the rookie was already the Celtics' best player that season. He averaged 21.3 points, 10.4 rebounds, 4.5 assists, and 1.7 steals in his first year in the NBA. He led Boston in scoring, rebounding, and steals while finishing second in assists. And though Magic Johnson was experiencing an excellent rookie campaign himself, Larry Bird was selected as the 1980 Rookie of the Year primarily because of how he turned the Boston Celtics from being a 29-win team to a 61-win squad on top of his excellent statistics. The Celtics were the top team in the NBA during the regular season.

As the Celtics immediately advanced to the second round of the playoffs, Bird and company had plenty of rest coming into their matchup with the Houston Rockets. They made quick work of the Rockets. Bird did not even have to explode for high-scoring games. Larry had 15, 14, and 18 points when the Celtics blew out the Rockets by 18, 20, and 19 in Games 1, 2, and 3, respectively. In the series clincher, Larry Bird went for 34 points as the Boston Celtics swept the Houston Rockets in four games.

In the Eastern Conference Finals, the rookie Bird would go for a classic battle with the veteran high-flying superstar Julius Erving of the Philadelphia 76ers. Erving's experience won out in Game 1 when he went for 29 points to lead the Sixers past Boston and Larry, who finished with 27 points. Bird bested his high-flying counterpart in Game 2 when he finished with 31 points to lead the Celtics to a win.

In another strong outing in Game 3, the two superstars battled it out with one another for playoff supremacy. In the end, Erving won the game to give the Sixers the series lead once again. Bird and Boston would fail to contain Dr. J in Game 4 when Philly went up 3-1 in the series with a 12-point win. In the end, Larry Bird's rookie campaign would end with an 11-point loss in Game 5. He finished with only 12 points and the Celtics lost the series to the 76ers. Ever the primetime performer, Bird upped his play in the playoffs of that season. He averaged 21.3 points, 11.2 rebounds, and 4.7 assists in the postseason.

## The Dawn of the Boston Big Three, First NBA Title

While drafting Larry Bird in the 1978 NBA Draft singlehandedly turned the Boston Celtics' fortunes around starting in 1979, it was the offseason trade that was made by Celtics executive Red Auerbach which ultimately made the team a dynasty. The Boston Celtics were the owners of the 1st and 13th pick of the 1980 NBA Draft primarily because of how

Auerbach maneuvered trades before Bird's arrival. Red then traded those picks over to the Golden State Warriors for the latter's 3rd pick and for rising 7-foot center Robert Parish. In the 1980 Draft, the Celtics would use the 3rd pick to bring over Kevin McHale from the University of Minnesota. Those offseason moves ushered in Boston Celtics' "Big Three" era.

The Celtics immediately became a force to be reckoned with because of the additions of those two frontcourt players despite losing longtime starting big man Dave Cowens to retirement. Parish brought a lot of rebounding and inside scoring for Boston. Meanwhile, the rookie Kevin McHale was a capable post scorer off the bench as either Parish's or Bird's backup at one of the frontcourt positions.

While Parish and McHale were both enjoying a good season in their first year in the Celtics' green uniform, the standout name and force remained Larry Bird. Bird would perform at the same rate as he did in his rookie season as he proved to the world that his first year in the NBA was not a fluke or a product of having no other superstar teammates. Bird continued to play at a superstar's rate while leading the Celtics to a 14-6 start through their first 20 games. He even led Boston to a 12-game winning streak in December. He had a highlight game of 35 points in a win against Chicago on December 13, 1980, to give Boston their fourth consecutive victory in that streak.

With Larry Bird playing at a steady rate while averaging more than 20 points and more than ten rebounds per game and while leading the Celtics to another strong regular season record, he was once again named to the Eastern Conference All-Star Team. Shortly after the All-Star break, he would go for 36 points in a rivalry game against the Los Angeles Lakers on February 11, 1981. That win sealed a season sweep against the Lakers, who they had defeated on January 18 in Boston. Unfortunately, Larry Bird could not face Magic Johnson that year because the star playmaker missed the majority of his games due to injury.

While Bird is known for his scoring and rebounding, it was during that season when he upped his assist rate because he had plenty of capable teammates to pass the ball to. From February 27 until March 3, he had four consecutive games of making 12 assists on top of his usual double-digit scoring. All four games were wins.

At the end of the regular season, Larry Bird averaged 21.2 points, 10.9 rebounds, 5.5 assists, and two steals while playing 39.5 minutes per game in 82 appearances. For the second consecutive season, he led the Celtics in scoring, rebounding, and steals while finishing second in assists again. With the additional help, the Celtics were once again the top team in the NBA with a record of 62-20.

The Boston Celtics were an automatic entry to the Eastern Conference semi-finals because of their position as the top seed in the East. The Celtics would meet the Chicago Bulls in the second round. While the games were not lopsided, Boston would end up sweeping the Chicago Bulls in four games. In Game 1, Bird scored 23 points. He was limited to 12 points in Game 2, but the Boston Celtics still took it by 9 points. His best performance of the series was 35 points in the series-clinching Game 4.

In the Eastern Conference Finals, Larry Bird and his Celtics would face the Philadelphia 76ers once again in a rematch of their 1980 bout. While Larry Bird finished Game 1 of that series with a 33-point outburst, it seemed like the 76ers would once again get the best out of the Celtics as they defeated the green team by a mere point. Bird would come back stronger by scoring 34 points in Game 2 while leading the Celtics to a series-tying 19-point win.

Similar to what happened in the 1980 Eastern Conference Finals, the Sixers would retake the series by taking Game 3 by 10 points. Philly would go up 3-1 in Game 4 with another win. In both of those losses, Larry Bird had mediocre outings. Because the Celtics were down 1-3 in the series, it seemed like the Sixers were on an impending second trip to the NBA Finals. But it was also at that moment when Larry Bird proved to be one of the most clutch players in NBA history.

Larry Bird would score 32 points in a tight Game 5. The Celtics would win that game to inch within one game of the Philadelphia 76ers series lead. In another strong outing in Philadelphia, the Boston Celtics would complete the series comeback by winning Game 6 by merely two points. With the series going to Game 7, all eyes were on Larry Bird and what he was about to do to give his team a Finals berth.

With Game 7 tied at 89 points and in the dying moments of the game, Larry Bird was in possession of the basketball with the whole world's attention on him. Bird ran the ball up the court with merely a second remaining on the clock. With the Sixers' defense still recovering, Bird went up for an awkward midrange shot that he released from his left hand. The shot managed to find the board, and it traveled all the way through the hole to give the Celtics a 91-89 lead. The Sixers had a chance to tie the game with two free throws, but only one found the end of the basket. Ultimately, the Boston Celtics were on their way to the

NBA Finals primarily because of that clutch play made by Larry Bird.

The Celtics would meet an underdog Houston Rockets in the NBA Finals. Everyone thought that it was going to be a relatively quick matchup because Boston had won the last 12 games against Houston. However, the Rockets fought hard. And as good as Larry Bird was throughout the postseason, the Rockets were able to put the clamps on the sophomore superstar. They even led at the halfway mark of Game 1.

It was also in Game 1 of that series against Houston that Larry Bird turned in another one of his best moments. Late in the final quarter, the Celtics were trailing by three points. Larry Bird shot a midrange shot from the right side of the perimeter. It was at that moment when he proved to be one of the smartest players concerning natural basketball instincts.

As soon as he released the shot, he immediately ran up to the right side of the basket, even before his shot had reached the rim. His instincts were correct as the ball could not find the mark, but Bird was right where he was supposed to be when he rose up for a split second put back. He caught the ball mid-air as his momentum traveled his body towards the baseline. Larry would move the ball to his off hand to flip it off the backboard for a basket. Everybody in the building was stunned by that move; even the great Celtic legend Bill Russell was in awe of what happened. Bird knew his shot would miss, and he knew where it was going to bounce off. And he knew what to do if he caught his missed shot. The momentum of that shot delivered Boston a slim four-point win in Game 1.

In Game 2, the Rockets' superstar Moses Malone, who was limited to 13 points in Game 1, went for 31 points and 15 rebounds to match Bird's efforts of 19 points and 21 rebounds. Houston would end their drought against the Celtics by winning that important game in Boston. The Rockets, knowing how much of a threat Larry Bird was, focused all of their defensive attention on the blue-collar white man from Indiana. Bird was limited to 8 points in that game. Luckily, Larry was not a one-man show. Role players Cedric Maxwell and Chris Ford stepped up to score in place of the usual stars of Bird, Parish, Archibald, and McHale. The Celtics went up 2-1 in the series.

Larry Bird would again struggle in Game 4 as Houston would not give him space to operate. This time, it was the Rockets' role players turn to step up. They would win Game 4 to tie the series up. After tying the series up with Boston, Houston's Moses Malone trash-talked and belittled the Celtics by saying that they, "ain't that good." Malone's words motivated the

Celtic role players again. They stepped up to score big with Larry Bird still struggling to score.

The motivated Celtics never let up in Game 6. They raced on to a big early lead against the Houston Rockets in the latter's home arena. Ever the supportive fans, the Houston crowd cheered their heroes on when the Rockets were trying to make a rally. Bird would finally break out of his slump in that game. He was an instrumental piece in quelling the Houston run. He quieted the crowd by feeding Cedric Maxwell, who was named the Finals MVP, a heartbreaking three-point shot in the final moments of the game. Boston would win the game by 11 points. The win delivered to them the franchise's 14th NBA trophy as well as Larry Bird, who was merely two years into his career as a professional, his first championship.

## Falling Short

The Boston Celtics started their title defense with basically the same group of guys that gave them their first NBA title since 1976. Of course, it was Larry Bird leading the way for a group of players hungry for more championships. It was also during that season that the Boston Big Three started slowly making its name. Robert Parish was integrating himself into the Celtics culture while Kevin McHale proved to be a good pick off the bench as a rapidly improving big man. With that kind of a trio leading the way, nobody could discount the Celtics as one of the powerhouses of that era.

Larry Bird would lead the Boston Celtics to a 13-2 start throughout the first 15 games of the season. Bird played fantastically in each of those games and was quickly rising through the ranks of the most elite players in a league, which featured names such as Kareem Abdul-Jabbar, Moses Malone, Julius Erving, and Magic Johnson.

On December 22, 1981, Larry Bird would go for a then-season high of 36 points in a win against the Cleveland Cavaliers. In January of 1982, the Celtic superstar would eclipse that mark by putting up 40 points on the Detroit Pistons led by then-rookie Isiah Thomas. After that game, Larry went for a scoring flurry in the next set of bouts after focusing on rebounding and distributing early in the season. He would average 30.8 points in the next six games. He would be named to his third consecutive All-Star appearance shortly after that.

After more than a full season of not seeing his rival Magic Johnson on an NBA floor, Larry Bird would have a rivalry match against the crafty playmaker on February 14. On a one-on-one basis, Magic would best his rival by posting 19 points to

Bird's 12. However, the Boston Celtics bested the LA Lakers by five points that game.

Near the tail end of the regular season, Larry Bird would lead the Boston Celtics to a 13-game winning streak. With that kind of a late-season flurry, the Celtics re-established themselves as the team to beat especially because they remained the title holders. Boston ended the season with a 63-19 record, which was even better than their record when they were crowned the NBA champions in the 1980-81 season.

Larry Bird averaged 22.9 points, 10.9 rebounds, 5.8 assists, and 1.9 steals per game during the regular season. He was named to the All-NBA First Team for a third consecutive season after being a member of it since his rookie season. Bird was also given his first All-Defense selection as a member of the Second Team. Larry was a close runner-up to the MVP award, which was brought home by Moses Malone.

In the Eastern Conference semis, Larry Bird was held down to a tight shooting series by the defensive-minded Washington Bullets. In Game 1, which the Celtics won, Bird was limited to merely 10 points on 3 out of 10 shooting. Though he was let loose to score 26 in Game 2, Larry Bird could not salvage a win from that output. Bird would combine for only 24 points in the next two games. Fortunately, his teammates stepped up to deliver the Celtics a 3-1 lead. Bird would close out the series in five games by scoring 26 points in the clincher. Though the win seemed relatively quick, it was not an easy win; the Bullets kept fighting in all five games.

For the third consecutive season, the Boston Celtics would face the Philadelphia 76ers in the Eastern Conference Finals. For a moment, it seemed that Bird and company had finally figured out their opponents' weakness. The Celtics would win Game 1 by 40 big points. Larry Bird was equally big in that game. He finished with a triple-double of 24 points, 15 rebounds, and ten assists. In that outing, the Celtics were in prime championship form in their quest for a consecutive title.

Unfortunately for the Celtics, the Sixers were also a team that was hungry for a title. Philly would beat Boston in Game 2 to tie the series up 1-1. Bird would try his best to muster a win in Game 3 and to put the Celtics up once again. He ended that game with a triple-double of 15 points, 13 rebounds, and 11 assists. Despite Larry's best efforts, Philadelphia would win the game by a slim margin. The Sixers would take a commanding 3-1 series lead by winning Game 4 by 25.

As he had done in the past season, Bird would try to get his team back from a 1-3 deficit against the same team they accomplished the feat against just a year ago. Larry had 20 points, 20 rebounds, and eight assists in Game 5 to put Boston within one game of the Sixers. Though he was limited to 14 points in Game 6, Larry collected 17 rebounds to contribute to a 13-point win and to deny the Sixers a chance to finish the series in Philadelphia.

With the comeback complete, all that the Boston Celtics had to do was to win Game 7 to accomplish the same feat they did during the 1981 East Finals. But the Philadelphia 76ers had learned from their past mistakes. They let loose an offense onslaught to stagger the Celtics on their home floor. Despite a near triple-double effort from Bird, who had 20 points, 11 rebounds, and nine assists, nobody could stop the Sixers from draining buckets. In the end, Philly won by 14 points to advance to the NBA Finals. They had eliminated the defending champions from contention.

Coming into the 1982-83 season, the Celtics kept their core players for another run at a title. Banking on the leadership of Larry Bird, who headed their three most important players, the Boston Celtics stormed to another quick start. They were 19-4 through their first 23 games of the season. Larry was not without some highlight performances during that strong opening run. He had 38 points and 12 rebounds in a win against the New Jersey Nets on November 7, 1982. In a battle against Isiah Thomas' Detroit Pistons on December 4, Bird had a triple-double of 30 points, 16 rebounds, and 12 assists. He then had 36 points and 19 rebounds when the Celtics collected their 18th win of the season.

It was during that season that the rivalry between Larry Bird and Magic Johnson blossomed. On January 30, 1983, the two superstars met in Boston. Bird would finish the game with 21 points, and Magic almost poured in a triple-double. The star point guard finished with 14 points, nine boards, and ten dimes. The game was not so hotly contested, though. The Celtics won by 15 points to draw first blood in their regular season series.

In the meantime, Larry Bird would see his fourth consecutive All-Star Game appearance. He was a no-brainer for a spot in the midseason classic because of how he elevated his numbers and his game year after year, and because of how he transformed the Boston Celtics into one of the best teams of that era. On his way to that fourth All-Star selection were several triple-double games and numerous clutch scoring outputs.

On February 23, Larry Bird and Magic Johnson would meet for the second time that season. The two superstars battled it out in what was to become great all-around efforts from both Bird and Johnson. Magic completed a triple-double output. He had 20 points, 13 rebounds, and ten assists. Meanwhile, Larry fell an assist short of that accomplishment. The legendary forward had 32 points, 17 rebounds, and nine assists to lead his team to a season sweep against their bitter rivals.

While Larry Bird poured in some memorable highlight games and some high-scoring outputs that season, nothing could top what he did on March 30, 1983. Larry would go for 53 big points in a 26-point blowout against the Indiana Pacers. He broke two records that night. First, he surpassed the franchise record of 51 points set by Sam Jones. That record had stood for 28 years before Bird broke it. Larry then set a franchise record of 24 points in a single quarter. He did that in the third quarter when the Celtics were blowing the Pacers away. Larry needed only 30 shots to reach his 53-point outburst. That goes to show how efficient of a shooter and scorer Bird was.

Larry Bird ended the season averaging 23.6 points, 11 rebounds, 5.8 assists, and 1.9 steals. Bird set new highs in both scoring and rebounding. He was named to the All-NBA First Team for the fourth consecutive season and to the All-Defensive Second

Team for the second straight time. Also for a straight season, Larry Bird lost out to, you guessed it, Moses Malone for the Most Valuable Player award. Nevertheless, the Celtics remained top contenders with a record of 56-26 entering the postseason.

Boston, as the third team in the East, faced the Atlanta Hawks in three games for a chance to qualify for the next round of the playoffs. That was the first time that Larry Bird would meet Dominique Williams in the postseason. It would not be the last, either. The two legends would battle it out in classic matches in future playoff bouts. In the meantime, the Celtics defeated the Hawks in three games. Bird averaged 22.3 points, 13.3 rebounds, and 7.7 assists. His only poor game was when he was limited to 15 points on 4 out of 18 shooting in a Game 2 loss.

The Celtics' luck ran out in the second round when they faced the Milwaukee Bucks. There was indeed reason to "Fear the Deer" as the Bucks blew Boston out in Game 1 by 21 big points. Unfortunately for Larry, he missed Game 2, which the Celtics also lost. Bird came back in Game 3 to deliver an amazing stat line of 21 points, 14 rebounds, six assists, and six steals. Despite his efforts, Milwaukee took a 3-0 series lead. The Bucks completed the sweep of the Boston Celtics by defeating them by 14 points in Game 4. That was Larry Bird and the Celtics' most disappointing playoff performance since the former joined the team in 1979.

## First MVP, Finals Battle with the Lakers, Second NBA Title

It was during the 1983-84 season that Larry Bird blossomed into arguably the best superstar the NBA had to offer. Of course, it was also during that season when he had his best battles with Magic Johnson, the other superstar with a claim to the throne of the NBA's greatest. But, as history would tell, it was to be one of Larry's finest seasons.

Bird started off the season on a high note, leading the Celtics to a record of 9-1 through their first ten games. Larry put up amazing stats through those games and filled up the sheets with his all-around style of play. He had 39 points, eight rebounds, five assists, and four blocks when he gave the Celtics their seventh win against Isiah's Pistons. When Boston got their ninth consecutive win, Bird posted a triple-double of 28 points, ten rebounds, and 11 dimes. Bird led his team to a 14-6 start. He had four triple-doubles in those first 20 outings.

On February 8, 1984, Larry Bird and the Boston Celtics met Magic Johnson and the Los Angeles Lakers for the first of two meetings that season. The two all-around stars managed to lead their respective teams in almost all the key statistical categories in that game. Larry had 29 points, 11 rebounds, and seven assists. Meanwhile, Magic posted 20 points, eight rebounds, and ten assists. But it was Johnson's six steals that stood out and gave the win to the Lakers.

A little more than two weeks later, Bird and Johnson would meet for the second time that season. Unlike their first meeting, Larry and Magic focused on getting the team involved in the scoring instead of trying to do their best to give their respective squads the victory. The Celtics leader had 14 points on only 12 shots. The Lakers playmaker only had 9 points. Los Angeles would win the bout thanks to the 18 assists of Magic Johnson, who swept Bird in the regular season for the first time since coming to the NBA.

Despite losing both rivalry games to Earvin Johnson, Larry Bird did not let up throughout the final stretches of the season as he led the Boston Celtics to another strong finish. The Boston Celtics ended the regular season with a record of 62-20. Once again, the Celtics were the top-seeded team in the Eastern Conference in the first season that the NBA allowed eight teams to qualify for the playoffs, and in the first season when the three-round elimination format was implemented.

Larry Bird posted season averages of 24.2 points, 10.1 rebounds, 6.6 assists, and 1.8 steals. The Celtic superstar was in the prime of his all-around powers, posting seven triple-doubles that season. Because of his accomplishments in leading the Celtics to the top seed in the East while also putting up incredible statistics, Larry Bird was named the NBA's Most Valuable Player for the first time in his career after finishing second to Moses Malone for the last two seasons. Along with that accolade, Bird was a member of the All-NBA First Team for the fifth consecutive season and was a selection to the All-Defensive Second Team for the third straight time.

While Larry was enjoying a fantastic season on a personal level, it did not mean that the other Celtic players were merely in the background. Both of the other members of the Boston Big Three were enjoying incredible seasons in their rights. Robert Parish was in his usual consistent form. The Chief posted 19 points per game while leading the Celtics in rebounding with 10.7 boards a night. Meanwhile, Kevin McHale was enjoying his then-best season as a pro. He improved his scoring to 18.4 points while averaging 7.4 rebounds, all that while starting only ten games. As the best bench player in the NBA, McHale was named the NBA's Sixth Man of the Year. All three of the Boston's Big Three were All-Stars that season. With that caliber of a superstar trio leading the Celtics, the NBA were put on notice that Boston was heading for a title run.

In the first round of the postseason, Larry and his Celtics met the Washington Bullets. Though the Bullets were merely the eighth seed in the East, they gave Boston a good fight. The Celtics would win Game 1 by only eight points. Bird had 23 points, seven boards, and 12 dimes in that outing. In Game 2, Larry had another double-double of 23 points, 12 rebounds, and six assists. His team would win by only three points in that outing. Boston would lose Game 3 in Washington thanks to a valiant effort from the Bullets. Despite another strong fight from Washington, the Celtics were finally able to proceed to the second round via another tight finish in Game 4.

Bird would go head-to-head with Bernard King, one of the best scorers the NBA had to offer that season when the Celtics faced off against the New York Knicks in the second round. The first two games seemed like an indication of what was to happen in the series. Boston won Games 1 and 2 in blowout fashion with Larry Bird posting high numbers. He combined for 60 points, 20 rebounds, and 16 assists in the firs two meetings of the series.

When the series shifted over to New York, the rabid fans cheered their hearts off to give life to the Knicks. The Knicks would win both games at home to tie the series at 2-2. That was in spite of Bird's 27.5 points and 11 rebounds in Games 3 and 4. Nevertheless, Larry would lead his team to a 22-point win in Game 5 before succumbing in Game 6 despite a 35-point output. The series was going to Game 7. It was time for Bird to fly once more to bring Boston to new heights.

Game 7 of their series against the New York Knicks turned out to be one of Larry Bird's finest moments. Larry put it on himself to bring the Boston Celtics back to the Eastern Conference Finals. He took every shot he could make and sank almost every one of those attempts despite the degree of difficulty in some of them. Scoring was not the only thing on Bird's agenda that night. He would grab every rebound he could get en route to 12 boards. He also got his teammates involved whenever the defense collapsed on him. Bird delivered ten dimes that night. He finished with 39 points, 12 rebounds, and ten assists in a Game 7 win for the Celtics.

In the Eastern Conference Finals, Larry Bird and the Celtics were looking to get revenge against the Milwaukee Bucks, the team that had swept them out of the playoffs just a season ago. They did just that. In Game 1, the revenge-hungry Boston squad blew the Bucks out by 23 points. With Bird posting 32 points, 13 rebounds, and seven assists, the Celtics took a 2-0 lead via a

15-point win. They would take an insurmountable 3-0 lead with a win in Game 3. Larry tried his best to sweep the Bucks in Game 4. He had 32 points, ten rebounds, and eight assists in that outing. However, Milwaukee avoided an embarrassing loss with a nine-point win. But, in the end, the green machine was on a roll. The Boston Celtics made their return to the NBA Finals with a win in Game 5.

Waiting for the Boston Celtics in the NBA Finals were their bitter rivals, the Los Angeles Lakers. It was a revival of a Finals rivalry that spanned all the way back to when Sam Jones and Jerry West were blasting away from the perimeter, and when Bill Russell and Wilt Chamberlain were wrestling each other in the paint. It was a battle between the two most storied franchises in the history of the NBA.

While the Celtics were the top-seeded team that boasted the presence of the MVP Larry Bird, the Los Angeles Lakers were a formidable team that ran their opponents to the ground with their fast offense. Moreover, the Boston Celtics could not beat the Lakers in their two-game regular season series. On paper, it seemed like the Celtics were the clear winners. But, in essence, it was an uphill battle considering that the Lakers had bested them throughout the season.

LA proved their mastery over the Celtics when they took Game 1. It was not Larry Bird's finest moment. He had 24 points and 14 rebounds, but shot just 7 out of 17 from the floor. With both teams battling to a stalemate in Game 2, an overtime period was necessary to determine a winner. The Celtics came out on top with a slim three-point lead. Bird finished with 27 points and 13 rebounds as his team tied the series at one game apiece.

With the series moving over to Los Angeles, the Lakers were not in the mood to give back home court advantage to the Celtics. LA used an enormous second half rally to take the life out of the Celtics. Magic finished the 33-point blowout with 14 points, 11 rebounds, and 21 incredible assists that paved the way for seven Laker players in double-digit scoring.

In Game 4, the Lakers had all the chances to take a 3-1 advantage that could have easily won the title for them. However, a clothesline committed by Kevin McHale on Kurt Rambis resulted in an all-out brawl. The incident gave the Celtics enough gas to force overtime. In the dying seconds of the extra period, Magic Johnson turned an all-important possession over. Bird, ever the hard worker, worked his butt off to get ahold of the ball. He then hit a fall-away shot over the outstretched hands of Johnson to win the game. Larry finished the game with 29 points and 21 rebounds, which included nine on the offensive end.

With the series tied at 2-2, the Boston Celtics got home court advantage back, hoping to get back the momentum they sorely needed to win the championship. Back at home in Game 5, the Celtics blew the Lakers out by 18 points. Larry Bird had 34 points and 17 rebounds in that win. Dubbed as the "Heat Game", Bird endured the high temperature because of a problem with the air-conditioning system.

The Lakers would manage to force Game 7 with a win in Game 6. The aging Kareem Abdul-Jabbar fueled that win with his 30-point output. In Game 7, the Boston Celtics went up to a double-digit advantage because of a strong rally that spanned from the second quarter up to the early part of the second half. The Lakers tried to mount a run that would have saved their chances at an NBA title. But the Celtics held on to win the championship in seven games with an eight-point win. Larry Bird, who had 20 points and 12 rebounds in Game 7, was named the Finals MVP of his second championship win with averages of 27.4 points, 14 rebounds, and 3.6 assists.

## Second MVP, Finals Rematch with the Lakers

The Boston Celtics would not revamp the lineup that brought them the NBA title during the 1983-84 postseason. Larry Bird, Robert Parish, and Kevin McHale were still leading other capable players such as Dennis Johnson, Cedric Maxwell, Danny Ainge, and Dennis Johnson. With that lineup, the Boston Celtics were still the title favorites, especially because they still had the crown atop their heads.

While the common belief is that a player has already reached his peak in an MVP season, Larry Bird showed in the 1984-85 season that he was yet to reach the height of his talents. He led the Celtics to an undefeated start through the team's first five games, averaging about 34 points in that span. His lowest output in that start was a 29-point game in a win against the Nets. He had 42 points versus the Philadelphia 76ers when the Celtics won their fifth straight game.

On November 15, 1984, Larry Bird would meet a young future superstar for the first time in their respective careers. That youngster was a 6'6" athletic guard playing for the Chicago Bulls, and his name was Michael Jordan. Jordan, similar to what Bird did in his rookie season, was dominating the league in just his first year. In his first game against Bird, he scored 27 points as opposed to the Celtic legend's 14 points. However, Larry did everything else better and led his team to a blowout win. At that moment, Bird was still the best player in the NBA, but would realize that Michael Jordan was going to be something else in years to come.

Larry Bird would have a classic matchup against Dominique Wilkins on December 9, 1984. The two superstars tried to one-up each other in a great shootout. Whatever Bird did, Wilkins tried to do better. Whenever Dominique would score, Larry would try to score on the other end as well. In the end, Larry and the Celtics came out with the win. Wilkins finished with 47 points. Meanwhile, Bird had 48 points and 14 rebounds. What was amazing was that he shot 20 out of 32 from the floor for a shooting clip of 62.5%.

As he continued to improve from his already great MVP season in 1984, Larry Bird played the role of an all-around player almost to perfection. He had three consecutive triple-doubles from December 26 to 29. All three games were wins. Nobody doubted that Bird was a great scorer and a phenomenal shooter. At that point of his career, there was no question that he had become the best all-around player in the NBA.

Bird would meet Magic in a rematch of the 1984 Finals on January 16, 1985. He finished with 19 points, 11 rebounds, and seven assists while helping to contain Johnson to 8 points. In contrast to the two teams' matchup during the 1984-85 regular season, the Celtics were able to beat the Lakers in their first meeting that season.

Barely a week after that game against the Lakers, Larry Bird would go for 48 points once again. He hit 17 of 28 shots against the Portland Trailblazers on January 27 while also grabbing ten rebounds and dishing out seven assists. The Celtics needed every bit of the points that Bird could put up because they won the game by only one point. That performance and ones similar capped off another All-Star season for Bird. That was the sixth consecutive trip to the midseason classic.

On February 17, Larry Bird and his Celtics would lose their second matchup with Magic and the Lakers that season. Bird finished with 33 points and 15 rebounds as he and Johnson split their two-game regular season series. The very next day, Larry bounced back by posting 30 points, 12 rebounds, ten assists, and nine steals for a triple-double game that almost became the first quadruple outing in the history of the NBA. He could have gone for that accomplishment if his team was not leading by more than 20 points in the fourth quarter.

Larry Bird would have his best single game performance at that moment of his career on March 12, 1985. Nine days prior, teammate Kevin McHale broke his franchise record for points when he scored 56. Larry Bird told the media that McHale could have and should have gone for 60 points. If his teammate could not do it, it was Larry's turn to do it. Bird scored 60 points against the Atlanta Hawks, the same team he scored 48 on earlier in the season. He went 22 out of 36 from the floor in that game and re-established himself as the Celtics' best single-game scorer. He gave McHale only nine days to hold the record.

At the end of the regular season, Larry Bird was named the season's MVP for the second consecutive season. The two-time NBA MVP elevated his game and numbers that season. Bird averaged 28.7 points, 10.5 rebounds, 6.6 assists, 1.6 steals, and a career-high 1.2 blocks. Larry had eight triple-doubles the entire season. He also shot a then-career high 52.2% from the floor while shooting a career-high 42.7% from the three-point line. With those numbers along with a 63-19 finish for the Boston Celtics, how could Bird not be named the Most Valuable Player?

Larry Bird continued his dominance into the postseason. In Game 1 of their first-round meeting with the Cleveland Cavaliers, Bird posted 40 points to lead the Celtics to a three-point lead. He then had 30 points in Game 2 to help his team go up 2-0 in the first round. The Boston Celtics capped a series sweep against the Cavaliers with a Game 3 win. Bird had 34 points, 14 rebounds, and seven assists in that series-ender, averaging 34.7 points, 10.7 rebounds, and 5.7 assists in the first round.

The MVP would lead his team to a 34-point win against Isiah Thomas's rising Detroit Pistons in Game 1 of their second-round matchup. He would then score 42 points while grabbing ten rebounds and dishing out six assists when the Celtics took a 2-0 lead in a better-fought Game 2. With those two wins at home, the Celtics were in prime position to get back to the Eastern Conference Finals.

The Detroit Pistons would take the series home for Games 3 and 4. In those two games, they were able to utilize their tough, physical defense to perfection in trying to hold back the Boston Celtics' stars. After basically dominating the league with his scoring, Bird was held to 23 points per game in the two losses in Detroit. When the Celtics went back to Boston for Game 5, Larry Bird broke out of a mini-slump. He had 43 points and 13 rebounds en route to a Boston victory. Despite a difficult shooting night from Larry Bird in Game 6, the Boston Celtics finished off the Detroit Pistons in six games to proceed to the Conference Finals for another season.

In the Eastern Conference Finals were two familiar foes for Larry Bird. Moses Malone and Julius Erving were two superstars that Larry had the pleasure of going up against in the postseason plenty of times in the past. Backing up the two veterans was an undersized but ultra-talented 6'6" rookie power forward named Charles Barkley. The Philadelphia 76ers, on paper, appeared to be just as talented as that year's edition of the Boston Celtics.

All the talent in the world could not save the Sixers from the Celtic machine. With the defense focused on him, Larry Bird dished out seven assists to help his teammates gain confidence in their shooting. Bird finished with 23 points in a Game 1 win. He then had 24 points, eight rebounds, and seven dimes when he led his team to a 2-0 series lead before going 3-0 in Game 3 with an 11-point win. Philadelphia would survive for at least one more game by winning Game 4. Despite a tough shooting night, Larry Bird did just enough to beat the Sixers in Game 5 en route to another appearance in the NBA Finals.

For the second consecutive season, Larry Bird would meet Magic Johnson and his LA Lakers in the NBA Finals. The straight championship showdown between the two arch-nemeses further contributed to the revival and rise in popularity of the NBA. Everyone was hooked on the best and fastest growing rivalry in professional sports. The popularity of the rivalry was further compounded when new NBA commissioner David Stern focused the league's marketing strategy on the Celtics and the Lakers, specifically on Larry and Magic.[vii]

The Boston Celtics showed why they were the defending champions in the opening game of the rivalry series. They blew the Lakers out by 34 points at the end of the contest. Bird only had to play 31 minutes and scored only 19 points in a game where every player in a green uniform seemed to hit their shots. No Celtic player had a bigger game that night than utility guy Scott Wedman, who scored 26 points while hitting 11 of 11 shots that included 4 out of 4 from the three-point line. The Lakers, however, would not let their rivals best them in consecutive outings. Kareem scored 30 points to match Bird's output to win the bout by seven points.

In Game 3 when the series moved over to Los Angeles, the Lakers were in prime form as they ran the Boston Celtics out of The Forum. Bird struggled in that blowout loss with 8 out of 21 for only 20 points. Never the high scorer, Magic Johnson went for 17 points and 16 assists to pave the way for guys like James

Worthy and Kareem Abdul-Jabbar. Like they always do, the Boston Celtics bounced back in Game 4. Bird finished the two-point win with 26 points and 11 rebounds while McHale and Dennis Johnson contributed high-scoring double-double outputs of their own to tie the series 2-2.

In the third consecutive game in Los Angeles, the Lakers would regain home court advantage by banking on the inspired performances of their superstars. Kareem went for 36 points while Worthy scored 33. It was Magic who, again, paced the victory with his 26 points and 17 assists. The Celtics' trio of superstars just could not match the Laker Big Three's output. Bird would only score 20 points in another poor outing. In Game 6, Larry tried to shoot his way out of a slump to force Game 7. He finished with 28 points on 12 out of 29 shots from the field in that game. All his efforts were in vain because the Laker superstars were in top form that series. The Celtics would cede their NBA title to the Los Angeles Lakers in six games.

## MVP Three-Peat, Third NBA Championship

The ensuing offseason after losing to the Lakers in the NBA Finals was a momentous one for Larry Bird, who was suffering elbow and finger injuries that caused him to struggle during the NBA Finals. Bird spent the whole summer nursing his injuries before he would suffer another one. Larry was always a blue collar worker that loved doing all the hard work himself. He was shoveling rocks off of his mother's yard to make way for a driveway and hurt his back in the process. While it was not the main reason, the back injury he suffered that offseason contributed to Bird's slow decline in later seasons.[viii]

The offseason was also a fruitful one for the Boston Celtics. Former champion and MVP Bill Walton, who had a history of health problems, was in the market for a good team that he could help chase a championship. The top teams he considered playing for were, of course, the Boston Celtics and the Los Angeles Lakers, who were not only battling each other for NBA supremacy, but for free agency dominance as well.

Walton, in the end, chose the Celtics primarily because of Larry Bird. Bird said that what was important for him was that Walton could play whenever he was healthy enough to do so. Meanwhile, the Lakers would only sign Walton if the doctors cleared him. After the agreement, the Celtics sent longtime forward and 1981 Finals MVP Cedric Maxwell over to the LA Clippers for Bill Walton. It was a risky move considering that Maxwell was their starting small forward and that Walton was injury-prone. As we will find out later, the gamble paid off.

With the acquisition of Bill Walton, Larry Bird moved over to the small forward spot to make way for former two-time Sixth Man of the Year Kevin McHale at the power forward position. With Parish at center, McHale at power forward, Bird at small forward, and Walton backing up the two big men up front, the Boston Celtics were fielding a terrifying lineup that would soon dominate the NBA landscape.

While Bird's back was troubling him that season, it did not slow him down at all en route to another one of his best seasons and one of the best seasons in NBA history. Larry would lead the Celtics to a 17-3 start through their first 20 games. In one of those wins, he had 47 points and 12 rebounds in a win against the Bad Boys Detroit Pistons squad. He also had two triple-doubles, which included another near quadruple-double, in that strong start to the season.

On January 18, 1986, Bird would go for another shootout with Dominique Wilkins. Larry always had a knack for putting up big games against the Atlanta Hawks. In that high-scoring output, he went for 41 points on 15 out of 27 shooting to pace the win versus Dominique, who had 36 points in that game. In the very next match, Larry went for 21 points, 12 rebounds, and seven assists as he led the Boston Celtics to a 15-point win against the Los Angeles Lakers in their first meeting since going up head-to-head in the 1985 NBA Finals.

Shortly after being selected as an All-Star for the seventh consecutive season, Larry Bird was chosen to participate in the first ever three-point shootout in the All-Star Weekend. The highlight of that event was when he walked into the locker room full of the NBA's best shooters before the contest got started. His exact words were, "I'm just trying to see who'll come second."[ix] Bird, always one to always back his words up, went on to win the inaugural three-point contest.

Shortly after the All-Star break, Larry went to Portland to deliver another memorable performance. It was also during that game when Bird proved that he could put up and make a shot in any situation and with any hand. He made seven left-handed shots in that game en route to 47 points, 14 rebounds, and 11 assists. He also made the game-winning shot after an overtime period.[ix]

Larry Bird would complete another season sweep of Magic Johnson and the Los Angeles Lakers on February 16. He had 22 points and 18 rebounds in that game. Bird would then have four triple-double outputs in the next six games, still proving to be one of the best if not the best all-around players in the NBA. On

March 10, he would go for 50 points on 18 of 33 shooting from the field in a one-point loss to the Dallas Mavericks. Eight days later, he scored 43 in a 30-point blowout win over the Cleveland Cavaliers. What was impressive about that output was the fact that he only played 29 minutes.

At the end of the regular season, Bird averaged 25.8 points, 9.8 rebounds, 6.8 assists, and two steals. He was once again a member of the All-NBA First Team and was named as the season's Most Valuable Player for the third consecutive season. He was only the third player at that time in NBA history to three-peat in the NBA award. The other two players were Bill Russell and Wilt Chamberlain. Up to that point, only Kareem Abdul-Jabbar, Bill Russell, Wilt Chamberlain, and Moses Malone won at least three MVP's. Michael Jordan and LeBron James would soon follow him in that accolade.

At that point in his career, there was almost no doubting that Larry Bird was the best player the NBA had to offer. He had the statistics and individual awards to back him up in that regard. His accomplishments as a team player also contributed. Bird consistently led the Celtics to 60-win seasons. In the 1985-86 season, the Boston Celtics won 67 games, which was the most they won in the Larry Bird era. As far as individual accolades and team accomplishments were concerned, Larry Bird was indeed the greatest player in the NBA at that time.

But Bird was not done carving what was to become his best season as an NBA player. He still had unfinished business in the playoffs. All of his individual success and the wins that his team earned would be for naught if he was to fail in leading the Boston Celtics to the summit of the NBA mountain that season. The first unlucky team standing in his way was the Chicago Bulls.

While the Boston Celtics easily won the series in three games, they had no answer for Michael Jordan in the first two games. Though Larry Bird was the best player in the NBA at that time, the sophomore MJ was steadily moving up the ranks of the NBA's best. He was gaining popularity and improving at rates faster than Larry and Magic ever did during their younger years. However, Jordan was a great individual player while Larry and Magic were terrific team leaders. Bird proved just that in that series against the Bulls.

In Game 1, Michael Jordan torched whichever unlucky soul was placed on him. He would go for 49 big points on 18 of 36 shots from the field. As good as he was, Mike was merely a one-man team going up against the best trio that the NBA had ever seen at that time. The combination of Bird, Parish, and McHale was too much to handle when they drew first blood.

If Jordan could not beat the Celtics by scoring 49 points, he tried his best to do so again by scoring a current playoff record of 63 points. For the second consecutive game, the Celtics simply had no answer to the scorching hot Michael Jordan. Jordan was 22 out of 41 from the field and was 19 out of 21 from the free throw line. Unfortunately for the soon-to-be Greatest of All-Time, the Celtics were too good of a team to lose in double-overtime. In Game 3, the Celtics pummeled MJ, who only scored 19 points. With Jordan struggling, the Celtics easily won the game and the series.

In stark contrast to their usual high-scoring explosive matchups in the regular season, Larry Bird and Dominique Wilkins were both shooting blanks in Game 1 of their second-round meeting. Wilkins scored only 13 points while shooting 4 out of 15 from the floor. Bird would only go for 16 points, but that was just enough for the victory. Bird, who had 36 points, and the Celtics took advantage of Dominique's struggles in Game 2 to get another win.

After two consecutive poor shooting performances, the Hawks' high-scoring and high-flying superstar finally got his groove back. Dominique Wilkins scored 38 points in Game 3 to give the Celtics a tough battle. Larry Bird, who scored 28 in that game, had other players backing him up. McHale and Ainge each scored more than 20 points to give Boston a 3-0 advantage heading into Game 4. Thanks to the 37 points of Wilkins, the Atlanta Hawks managed to live for another day. Their hopes ended when Larry Bird scored 36 points to help the Celtics win the series by 33 points.

The Milwaukee Bucks did not give the Boston Celtics much of a fight in the Eastern Conference Finals. The Celtics would sweep the Bucks in four games. Three of those wins were in double digits as the Boston Celtics proved how much of a dominant team they were heading into their third consecutive NBA Finals appearance.

Unlike the last two NBA Finals, there were no Los Angeles Lakers waiting to give another classic series to the Celtics. The LA Lakers reached as far as the Western Conference Finals but were soundly and convincingly defeated in five games by the Houston Rockets led by the young twin tower combination of Hakeem Olajuwon and Ralph Sampson. But no matter how tall the task was, Larry Bird and his Celtics were ready to topple any skyscraper on their way to the NBA title.

Bird opened the Finals series by making sure his teammates were involved on the offensive end. Six Celtic players were in double-digit scoring at the end of the game, and all five of the starters had at least 18 points. Bird finished the Game 1 victory with 21 points, eight rebounds, and 13 dimes. While Game 1 was a little lopsided, Game 2 was not even close. Bird would lead five Boston players in double digits as their defense smothered the towering presence of Olajuwon and Sampson. Larry finished the 22-point win with 31 points.

The Houston towers suddenly got going when the series moved over to the Rockets' home court. Hakeem focused on the scoring while Ralph dominated the rebounds to discredit the efforts of the Boston Celtics' big men. Though Larry Bird recorded a triple-double performance of 25 points, 15 rebounds, and 11 assists, the Houston Rockets got away with a slim victory. Bird would once again showcase what it meant to be an all-around player when he narrowly missed a triple-double in Game 4, which the Celtics took from the Rockets to go up 3-1 in the series.

Everyone has bad nights. That even includes players with the transcendent skills and talents of Larry Bird. Bird would have an off performance in Game 5, which was a night when the Rockets seemed like they could not miss from the floor. With a blowout win, Houston inched within a game closer to the Celtics. But Larry Bird was not about to let his foes tie the series up and force Game 7. Bird's body language, defensive intensity, and on-court ferocity in Game 6 all seemed to indicate that he wanted to end the series right then and there. He put on another masterclass about what it meant to close out a series. Larry recorded his second triple-double of the series with 29 points, 11 rebounds, and 12 assists.

But his numbers could not give justice to the jaw-dropping display he put on that night. Celtic head coach KC Jones would say that "Larry Bird is where he wants to be." True enough, Bird was everywhere on the floor that night. He played with so much passion and heart that the Rockets' Jim Peterson even said that Bird took on five players by himself and still managed to score. At the end of the series, Larry almost averaged a triple-double. In six games, he averaged 24 points, 9.7 rebounds, and 9.5 assists. His performance earned him a second Finals MVP on top of a third NBA Championship. Bird gave the Boston Celtics the franchise's league-leading 16th NBA championship.

## 50-40-90 Season, Last Finals Appearance

By a trade two years before that Red Auerbach orchestrated with the Seattle SuperSonics, who were awful in the past season, the Boston Celtics were in position to make their already dominant team into a stronger dynasty with the second pick in the 1986 NBA Draft. With that pick, they selected Len Bias, an athletic forward from the University of Maryland.

Bias could have been the star that would have carried the Celtics as the Big Three aged. The franchise had their hopes on the young 6'8" collegiate star. However, things turned around quickly. Len Bias was found dead due to substance abuse just two days after the Celtics drafted him. It was a big blow to both the franchise and to Larry Bird, who could have had a young player to mentor and to pass the leadership baton to.

Nevertheless, the Boston Celtics still had Larry Bird and the rest of the Big Three to lead the team to greatness once again. True enough, Bird did just that. He led his team to another great start to the season as the Celtics went nearly 14-6 throughout their first 20 games of the season. In that span, Larry Bird had eight games of scoring at least 30 points while maintaining his penchant for doing everything else on the floor, whether it was rebounding, assisting, or defending. Unfortunately, one of those 20 games was a loss to their rivals, the Los Angeles Lakers.

On January 23, 1987, Bird would have another solid game against the Atlanta Hawks, a team he has always had a knack for scoring big on. He had 40 points and 12 rebounds while shooting 14 out of 24 in a 20-point win. A little over a month later while making another All-Star appearance and winning the three-point shootout for the second time, Bird would score a new season high of 43 points in a win against the Portland Trailblazers. He also had ten rebounds and eight assists in the process of putting on a masterful display on offense.

On March 20 to 22, Larry Bird would score back-to-back games of scoring at least 40 points. He first had 42 points and 12 rebounds in a win over the SuperSonics before going for 40 points and 13 dimes on the New Jersey Nets in another victory. At the tail end of the season, Larry would score a new season high of 47 points in a game against the New York Knicks in a double-digit win. He made 22 of his 34 field goal attempts in that game.

At the end of another great all-around season, Larry Bird was selected to the All-NBA First Team for the eighth consecutive season. He averaged 28.1 points, 9.2 rebounds, a career high 7.6 assists, and 1.8 steals. He also shot 52.5% from the field, 40% from the three-point line, and 91% from the foul stripe. With those kinds of shooting percentages, Larry Bird became the inaugural member of what was to become the 50-40-90 Club, a term used for players who average at least 50% from the field,

40% from the three-point area, and 90% from the free throw line. Only six other players would later join the 50-40-90 Club. That simply goes to show how great of a shooter Larry Bird was from any part of the arena.

Larry Bird and his top-seeded Boston Celtics opened the postseason by winning a tight Game 1 against the Chicago Bulls. In that match, Bird would only attempt seven shots from the field while focusing his energy on playing defense and making plays for teammates. He finished with 17 points, nine rebounds, and 13 assists. While he was instrumental in holding back Michael Jordan for an offensive explosion in Game 1, Bird would focus on putting points up on the board for his team that went 2-0 despite a 42-point outburst from Mike. Bird's 32 points and 14 rebounds were key in helping his team sweep the Chicago Bulls in three games.

In Game 1 of their second-round series against the Milwaukee Bucks, Larry Bird displayed his offensive virtuosity by scoring 40 points along with 11 rebounds, seven assists, and four steals in a 13-point win. He would have another steady output in Game 2 as he and his Celtics went up 2-0 in the series.

The Bucks would manage to win Game 3 in Milwaukee while holding Bird to 18 points. Bird would not let that bad game pull him and his team down. He would lead his team to a double-overtime victory in what was one of the best games of that year's playoffs. He finished with 42 points, seven rebounds, and eight assists in a 56-minute campaign.

A 3-1 series lead does not always mean a guaranteed spot in the next round. The Celtics proved that back in 1981 when they came back from a deficit against the Sixers. The Bucks attempted to be the next team to return from that seemingly insurmountable deficit. They would win Games 5 and 6 in high-scoring affairs and would force Game 7 after winning Game 6. Unfortunately for the Bucks, Larry Bird was still one of the most clutch players in the NBA. He led the Celtics with 31 points, ten rebounds, and eight assists in a game in which he did not even rest for a single second. Bird never spared a moment to sit down, believing that he was needed to will his team to a win. He did just that; his team was heading to defend their Eastern Conference throne.

The Celtics' reign as the Eastern Conference Kings would face some stiff and physical competition with the rise of the Bad Boys from the Detroit Pistons. Isiah Thomas led a physical team that had Larry Bird shooting 7 out of 22 in Game 1. Nevertheless, Bird had 16 rebounds and 11 assists to go along with his hard-earned 18 points to lead the Celtics to a 13-point win. Bird would manage to shake away Detroit's defense to score 31 points together with nine boards and 12 dimes in a Game 2 win.

Not letting their experienced champion opponents get the best of them, the Detroit Pistons buckled down on defense to smother not only Larry Bird but the rest of the Celtics in Games 3 and 4. Larry was limited to a combined effort of only 33 points on 14 out of 30 shooting from the field in the two losses in Detroit as the Pistons tied the series with two convincing victories on their home floor.

Bird would bounce back in Game 5 with one of the most memorable defensive plays in NBA history. The Detroit Pistons were up by a point with a few seconds left. Unfortunately for the Celtics, the Pistons had possession of the ball and their best passer was the one making the inbound play. Isiah Thomas was about to make the inbound pass to Bill Laimbeer to seal away the win and possibly close the series out in Detroit come Game 6.

Lo and behold, it was Larry Bird to the rescue. Ever the crafty defender with an eye that could see every possible play on the floor, Larry left his man to go for an interception of the inbound pass. His momentum almost carried him out of bounds, but Bird had enough wherewithal to throw the ball over to a streaking Dennis Johnson, who made the go-ahead layup with only a second remaining.[ix] That play saved the Celtics' season. The Pistons won Game 6 only to lose Game 7 to the defending champs in Boston.

For the third time in their storied rivalry, Larry Bird would meet Magic Johnson in the NBA Finals for another epic battle for league supremacy. It was going to be the rubber match. Larry and the Boston Celtics won round one while Magic and his Los Angeles Lakers got the second bout. While it would not be an indication of who was the better player, the winner of the 1987 NBA Finals would have bragging rights over the other.

It seemed like Magic and his team were hungrier for another title from the get-go. The Lakers ran circles around the Boston defense while Johnson used his top playmaking skills to get easy baskets for his teammates. Larry Bird would try and fight the Laker juggernaut. He finished the game with 32 points. But the Lakers ended Game 1 with a double-digit win. Johnson had 29 points, eight rebounds, and 13 assists.

The wear and tear of facing the physical defenses of the Milwaukee Bucks and the Detroit Pistons seemed to have taken a toll on the Boston Celtics, who went down 0-2 in the series after the Lakers soundly defeated them in Game 2. The injuries aggravated by the tougher road he took to get to the NBA Finals slowed down the once spry and agile 6'9" white man named Larry Bird. He would have 23 points and ten rebounds in Game 2. Meanwhile, his rival had 22 points and 20 assists.

Though they were down 0-2 in the series, Larry Bird always had a competitive spirit and an unerring determination to win. He went out to lead the Boston Celtics to a six-point victory on their home floor. Bird had 30 points and 12 rebounds in Game 3 to cut the Lakers' series lead to one game. He would go on to say that Game 3 was the most important game of the series for the Boston Celtics since they would have never had a chance had they lost that one.

Fueled by their win in Game 3, Larry and his Celtics went into Game 4 to battle the Lakers in what seemed to be the most hotly-contested game of the series. The Celtics were leading throughout the first three-quarters of the match. The Lakers, not willing to let their rivals tie the series up, stormed back in the fourth quarter to take a one-point lead with merely a few seconds left on the clock.

Larry Bird would then have one of his most clutch moments in those final seconds. With the ball in possession of the Celtics, the inbounder could not get the ball to Bird, who was tightly guarded by the Lakers' James Worthy by actually holding on to him with a fist full of the Celtic legend's jersey. Danny Ainge had no choice but to receive the inbound. As Worthy came out to help Ainge, Larry got a few moments to get open and to spot up on three. Ainge found him at that spot. As usual, Bird hit a clutch three-pointer to get his team up by two with only 12 ticks left on the clock.

While Larry Bird was one of the most clutch players the NBA could offer in that era, Magic Johnson was just as clutch. There was a reason why Larry and Magic were considered the best players of the 80's, and a reason why Bird and Johnson were archrivals. With the Lakers down by a point via a free throw made by Kareem Abdul-Jabbar, Los Angeles got hold of the ball once again because of a controversial turnover on the part of the Celtics. Magic was in possession of the ball with seconds remaining. Knowing he had the advantage over McHale on the perimeter, he drove to the basket and put up an impossible-looking hook shot from the perimeter to get over the outstretched arms of both of the Celtics' big men. The shot found its mark to give the Lakers a one-point lead with two seconds left.

Larry had one last chance to get the win. He would get the ball beyond the three-point line just in front of the Lakers bench. Larry would go for an off-balanced shot as time expired. Surprisingly and unfortunately, Bird's last-second attempt did not find the bottom of the basket. If there was a crucial turnaround moment in the series, it was the final seconds of Game 4.

Not ready to go quietly into the night despite facing a 1-3 deficit in the championship round, Larry Bird had 23 points and 12 rebounds to lead the four other Celtic starters, who all scored at least 21 points to win Game 5 by 15 points and to have another crack at tying the series. But that was all the fight that the Boston Celtics could give to their archrivals. Larry Bird was clearly hampered by his injuries and the physical toll of a tough playoff run. He was limited to 16 points on 6 out of 16 shooting in Game 6 when the Lakers finally defeated them for the championship in Los Angeles. That loss to the Los Angeles Lakers in the 1987 Finals signified the end of the Celtics' run as the top dogs in the NBA, and it was the last time Larry Bird would ever face Magic Johnson in the Finals.

## Second 50-40-90 Season, End of the Reign as the Kings of the East

Coming into the 1987-88 season, Larry Bird was still 30 years old and supposedly had plenty of years left playing at an elite level. However, his back issues began to get worse. Despite that, Bird was still one of the best, if not the best, players in the NBA at that time. He began to rely more on his fundamentals rather than his relentless attacking style. Bird started to shoot more from the perimeter and the three-point line than ever before. The new style did not hurt him; he had his best shooting and scoring season.

Larry Bird opened the season leading the Celtics to six straight wins. As early as the season was, Bird came out firing on the offensive end. In just the second game of the season for Boston, Larry went for 47 points on 19 out of 29 shooting against a fighting Washington Bullets team. Four days later on November 11, 1987, Larry took the Indiana Pacers to school for his first ever 40-20 game. Bird finished with 42 points and 20 rebounds in a dominant win.

It was during that season that Larry Bird had to take and make more shots to supplement the Boston Celtics' offense because starters Dennis Johnson and Robert Parish, who were both reliable scorers in their prime years, were already slowing down. As such, Bird had to bail the team out by trying to score more than he ever had. That season, Larry Bird had more 40-point games than he ever had throughout his career. Against the same Washington Bullets squad that he scored 47 on earlier in the season, Larry scored 49 points on January 27, 1988. He would reach that number again on February 15 just two weeks after he made another All-Star appearance and won the three-point shootout for a third consecutive season. In his final game of the regular season, he even outscored the then two-time scoring champion Michael Jordan, who finished with 39 points. Bird had 44 in that win.

At the culmination of the regular season, Larry Bird averaged a new career-high of 29.9 points together with 9.3 rebounds, 6.1 assists, and 1.6 steals. After posting shooting clips of 52.7%, 41.4%, and 91.6% from the field, the three-point line, and the free throw stripe respectively, he became a member of the 50-40-90 club for the second consecutive season. Bird was still the league's best small forward after he was named to the All-NBA First Team for the ninth and final time. He would also finish second to Michael Jordan in the MVP voting after leading the Boston Celtics to the top seed in the East with a record of 57-25.

Larry Bird was the catalyst for the first two dominant victories over a rising New York Knicks squad in the first round of the playoffs. He averaged 32.5 points when the Boston Celtics blew the Knicks out in Games 1 and 2. The Knicks managed to live for another day when they won Game 3 in New York. The series would end in Game 4 when Bird scored 28 points.

Larry has historically been a good scorer against the Atlanta Hawks. That trend did not change in Game 1 of their second-round meeting. The Celtic legend went for 38 points on 15 out of 25 shooting from the field when Boston drew first blood. Bird would not attempt a lot of shots in Game 2, which the Celtics won to go up 2-0 in the series. He finished with only 16 shots on 14 field goal attempts.

The Hawks got their groove back when they went home to Atlanta for Games 3 and 4. They would blow the Boston Celtics out of the building by 18 points. On top of that, they let Larry Bird bleed for his 22 points that he earned by shooting 5 out of 18 from the field. The home dominance continued for the Atlanta Hawks. Banking on a good second quarter and the terrific 40-point performance of Dominique Wilkins, the Hawks tied the series 2-2 against the dominant Boston Celtics dynasty team. They would then surprise the world in Game 5. Holding

Bird to a relatively low scoring performance again, the Hawks took Game 5 in Boston to go up 3-2.

With Larry Bird and the Celtics in the midst of an elimination game, the Green Team held on to defeat the Hawks in Atlanta when the latter had all the chances to eliminate Boston to proceed to the Eastern Conference Finals. The series was set to go to Game 7, and it was going to be a showdown between the two teams' superstars—Larry Bird and Dominique Wilkins.

Wilkins would come out of Game 7 smoking. He could not seem to miss from the floor on his way to a game-high 47 points. Larry Bird was not about to let someone outshine him. Bird engaged the younger and more athletic Human Highlight Reel in a shootout worthy of being called one of the best one-on-one battles in the annals of the NBA. Larry did his best to match Dominique's output. Bird made 9 of his ten shots in the fourth quarter to score 20 points.[vi] He ended the game with 34 points on 24 shots. Though Bird's performance was a little less fantastic compared to Wilkins', the former did just enough to secure the Boston Celtics a win and another appearance in the Eastern Conference Finals.

In the way of Bird's possible fifth straight appearance in the NBA Finals were the physically-imposing Detroit Pistons squad that ran enemies into the ground with their pounding and smothering defense. Their defensive strategy would frustrate Larry Bird early in the series. Bird was held to a relatively low 20-point performance on 8 out of 20 shooting when the Pistons took Game 1 in Boston. It would take the Celtics two extra periods just to deny Detroit of two steals on the former's own home floor. Despite playing 54 minutes, Larry Bird was evidently smothered and bothered by the Detroit defense. He was held to 18 points on 6 out of 20 shooting.

The offensive frustrations continued for Larry Bird in Game 3. He just could not shake off the Pistons physical defense and went 6 out of 17 from the floor for only 18 points. The Pistons would take the series lead back with a win in Game 3. In a very low-scoring game for such a high-octane team like the Boston Celtics, Bird would somehow lead his team to a one-point win despite playing at a pace that favored the Detroit Pistons.

Back in Boston for Game 5, Larry Bird would have his best individual performance of the series. He had 27 points, 17 rebounds, and five steals in another game that saw him struggling from the field. Bird was 9 out of 25 from the floor. Despite scoring his best performance of the series that game, the Celtics could not stop Isiah Thomas from scoring at will. Detroit went up 3-2 after that win. In Game 6, the Boston

Celtics were finally dethroned as the best team in the Eastern Conference in a game where Larry Bird shot 4 out of 17 from the field.

For the first time since 1983, the Boston Celtics were not the representatives of the Eastern Conference in the NBA Finals. The Detroit Pistons came into the series with the perfect game plan. They smothered and defended Larry Bird to perfection. Bird was held to 19.3 points on 35% shooting from the field after averaging nearly 30 points the entire regular season. The struggles from the floor were a combination of the Pistons' tough physical defense and the toll that Larry's injuries had endure that season. Nevertheless, what that series against the Detroit Pistons proved was that Larry Bird was the barometer of that Boston Celtics squad. The Celtics could only go as far as Bird could take them.

## Injury Season

Larry Bird was coming off a disappointing Eastern Conference Finals loss at the hands of the Detroit Pistons, and the disappointments and setbacks did not stop. He came into the 1988-89 season hobbling because of the injuries he had suffered throughout his storied career. While Bird opened the season strong when he had 29 points, five rebounds, five assists, and four blocks in a win over the Knicks in his first game of the season, there seemed to be something wrong with him as the season went on. He would only play a total of six games that season after undergoing surgery to remove bones spurs that were troubling both of his heels. Larry Bird would not play again that season. The Celtics were only 42-40 that year.

## Return from Injury, First Round Exit

Larry Bird came back healthy and vigorous for the 1989-90 season. He would prove that by posting 50 points on the Atlanta Hawks on November 11, 1989, when the Boston Celtics won by 11 points. Larry was 19 out of 25 from the field and 11 out of 12 from the foul stripe in that excellent performance. He would once again have a classic Larry Bird performance on December 13. Bird went for 40 points, 11 rebounds, and ten assists in a triple-double effort when he led his team to a double-digit win against the Seattle SuperSonics. A week later, he had 40 points against Karl Malone and the Utah Jazz in a win.

At the age of 33 years old, Larry Bird was still looking spry and active though he was clearly hampered by a bad back and slowed down by the wear and tear of the NBA game. Nevertheless, he was still named as an All-Star while continuing to dominate the league in a way only Larry Bird can. Bird would score 46 points together with eight rebounds and ten assists in a win over the Orlando Magic on March 16, 1990. That performance was merely five days after he dropped 41 on the Sixers. Larry would have a total of seven games of scoring at least 40 points that season. He also had ten triple-doubles as he proved that he was back in shape and form after technically missing the entire 1988-89 season.

Bird averaged 24.3 points, 9.5 rebounds, 7.5 assists, and 1.4 steals in his 11th season as an NBA professional. After dominating the league as the NBA's best small forward for a decade, Larry Bird was demoted to the All-NBA Second Team that season. But there was no denying he was still one of the NBA's best forwards and leaders particularly since he led the Boston Celtics to a record of 52-30 after the team went for only 42 wins without him.

In the playoffs, Larry Bird was in prime form to wreak havoc like he used to do when he was in his prime playing years. He had 24 points, 18 rebounds, and ten assists for a triple-double game in their first outing against the New York Knicks in the postseason. He would help the Celtics get a 2-0 series lead when he was a key player in the 29-point win in Game 2. He had 15 points and 16 dimes in that win. Things would quickly turn sour for the Boston Celtics and Larry Bird. The younger Knicks used the momentum of their two home wins in Games 3 and 4 to get rid of the Celtics in Game 5. It was the first time that Larry Bird was eliminated in the first round of the playoffs.

## Injury-Prone Season, Beginning of the End of a Legendary Career

Larry Bird would come into the new 1990-91 NBA season as a hobbling 34-year old veteran. His back problems were slowing him down and preventing him from dominating in the way he used to before nagging injuries got the best of him. His other Big Three teammates were not in good shape, either. McHale went back to the bench as head coach Chris Ford opted to preserve him because age and injuries were also slowing him down. Despite performing well for a 37-year-old center, Robert Parish was not a player that the Boston Celtics could count on to carry the team night in and night out. The only bright spot was the improving youngster Reggie Lewis (now deceased).

Bird would not let age or injuries prevent him from putting up fantastic shows on the floor. On November 14, 1990, in a win against the Charlotte Hornets, Bird put up 45 points, eight boards, eight assists, and five blocks in a game that featured the Larry Legend of old. On December 5, he would then score 43 points together with eight rebounds and 13 dimes in a win over the Denver Nuggets. Bird was selected to his 12th overall All-Star appearance after he valiantly continued to lead the Celtics in all facets of the game. Unfortunately for him, Larry would miss a total of 22 games because of nagging back injuries.

At the end of the 1990-91 season, Larry Bird's scoring numbers dropped considerably to an all-time low not counting the 1988-89 season. He averaged only 19.4 points on a career-low 45.4% shooting clip. He also averaged 8.5 rebounds and 7.2 assists while showing the world that he was still one of the best all-around performers in the NBA. Bird was not selected to an All-NBA Team that season. Nevertheless, he led the Boston Celtics to a record of 56-26, which was good for the second seed in the Eastern Conference.

Though clearly hobbled by injuries, Larry Bird did just enough to lead the Boston Celtics past the Indiana Pacers in Game 1 of their first-round series against the Indiana Pacers. Though he shot 6 out of 20 for 21 points, he recorded a triple-double with his 12 rebounds and 12 assists. After another tough shooting night in Game 2, the Boston Celtics would drop one game at home before gaining home court advantage back in Game 3. Bird combined for only 11 out of 31 from the floor in those two games.

The Pacers would force Game 5 by winning Game 4 in Indiana. Larry Bird would only have 18 points in another mediocre game for the former three-time NBA MVP. Though nearing the age of 35, Larry Bird's mentality as one of the league's best clutch performers never changed. He would have 32 points, nine rebounds, and seven assists to help the Celtics eliminate the Pacers in the first round. He shot 12 out of 19 from the floor in that game. The only knock on his shooting clip that night was that he could not make any of his five attempts from beyond the three-point line.

Larry Bird's Detroit nightmare would haunt him in the second round when the Boston Celtics faced the Pistons. He could never solve the smothering defense that the Pistons masterfully put on him. Bird was limited to 16 points on 7 out of 15 from the field in Game 1. Luckily, the Celtics came out with a win. Game 2 was another tough one for Larry as he was held to ten points on a bad shooting night. Fortunately, the rest of the Celtics stepped up and blew out the Pistons by 32 big points.

Though they won Games 1 and 2 on their home floor, Larry Bird was clearly not the same dominant player he used to be. He would struggle from the field through Games 3 to 5. He would only shoot 15 out of 42 in those three games, which were all losses. The Celtics were eliminated in Game 6, a night that Larry Bird missed due to his nagging injuries.

## Final NBA Season

In the offseason, Larry Bird would undergo surgery to remove a disc in his back because he had been suffering from a compressed nerve. Though surgery fixed the injury, the pain would never go away. The nagging pain combined with Larry Bird's advanced age in NBA years were all factors in his decision to retire. Unknown to him and the whole world, the 1991-92 season would become Bird's final season as a professional.

Larry Bird would never regain the form he had during the middle of the 1980's wherein he was so dominant that he was regarded as the best player in the NBA. However, he did still show flashes of what was once a brilliant professional basketball player. He had 32 points and 11 rebounds in a win over the Orlando Magic on November 27, 1991. Larry then put up 31 points, 12 rebounds, and seven assists in a win against the Knicks on December 6. However, shortly after that, Bird would miss a total of 37 games because of the resurfacing injuries. But that did not stop him from getting selected as an All-Star. It was his 12th and final selection for an All-Star squad.

The aging Celtic legend would come back in March of 1992. At that point, he was but a shell of his former self as he struggled to put up baskets despite playing his usual all-around style of basketball. But, for a single night, the Larry Bird of old returned for a final legendary performance. It was a night to behold for all basketball fans, whether they hated him or adored him.

The clutch Larry Bird was on full display in the fourth quarter of a game against the Portland Trailblazers on March 15, 1992. Bird pulled off a fourth quarter performance that was one for the ages. He scored the Celtics' final nine points and a total of 16 points in that period to force overtime against the top Western Conference team. But Bird was not only scoring, he was making plays and grabbing rebounds on his way to leading his team to a double-overtime victory in front of a faithful Boston crowd. He played so well that even Portland's Clyde Drexler was in awe of what happened.[iv]

Larry ended the game with 49 points, 14 rebounds, and 12 assists. That would be his final game of scoring at least 40 points. It was also his last triple-double and 59th triple-double of his all-around career. Bird ranked fourth in career triple-doubles at that time. Only Jason Kidd would subsequently surpass him in that regard. No other player in the history of the NBA has ever scored more points while piling up a triple-double.[ix]

Larry Bird ended that season averaging 20.2 points, 9.6 rebounds, and 6.8 assists in 45 appearances. He would lead the Boston Celtics to a record of 51-31, which qualified them for the second seed in the 1992 playoffs. Larry missed the entire first round of the postseason, but fortunately, the Celtics held the fort without him when they swept the Pacers in the opening series. Bird would only play four times in the second round matchup against the Cleveland Cavaliers. Three of those appearances were losses. The Cavs would beat the Celtics in seven games. In what was Larry Bird's final playoff appearance, he averaged only 11.3 points, 4.5 assists, and 5.3 rebounds.

## 1992 Olympics: The Dream Team

The 1992 Olympics held in Barcelona, Spain was the first time that the United States assembled a team of NBA players to send over to the Olympic basketball tournament. Larry Bird joined an ensemble that featured the likes of Magic Johnson, Michael Jordan, and Charles Barkley, among other great players. Chuck Daly was selected to coach the team that was described as "the greatest collection of basketball talent on the planet".[x]

In the tournament proper, Larry Bird scored had 14 points, four rebounds, three assists, two steals, and two blocks in the Dream Team's first game, which was against Spain. They won by 41 points. He would have 5 points and six rebounds in the 44-point demolition job over Brazil. Bird's finest game of the tournament came against Germany. He had 19 in that 53-point win.

Larry would then be content playing the part of a role player until the tournament's conclusion. The Dream Team unquestionably won the gold medal after decimating their opponents by an average of 44 points. Bird averaged 8.4 points, 3.8 rebounds, and 1.8 assists the entire tournament.

Shortly after the Olympics, Larry announced his retirement from the NBA game. The decision came after contemplating that his body could no longer handle the grind of another grueling 82-game NBA season.[iv] Bird retired as a winner like he had always been in his 13-year career. Winning the Olympic gold medal in his final organized basketball game was the best possible way he could have ended his NBA career.

# Chapter 5: Life After Retirement

## Boston's Special Assistant

The first five years of Larry Bird's post-NBA life was one spent mostly in the background, relaxing on the beaches of Florida and playing golf to pass the time. On paper, he was given the role of special assistant by the Boston Celtics' front office. The job carried only a few roles. He did some scouting and a few evaluations for five years. But Bird was always a competitor. He wanted the thrill of competing in any way possible. When he was finally ready to take on a bigger role with the Celtics, the front office took a different turn by hiring Rick Pitino as the new president and head coach. Because of that, Bird changed his career path.[iv]

## Coaching the Indiana Pacers

Larry Bird was always one of the brightest basketball minds on the court during his tenure as a player. He could see every play on the floor whether it was on offense or defense. That high basketball IQ and feel for the game helped him get a lot of assists, rebounds, and steals on both ends of the floor. While his offensive skills were his best tools in forging a legendary career, his basketball smarts were what got him to the dance in the first place.

As a basketball coach, Bird's skills and capabilities in that field were yet to be tested. He had never tried coaching even at the lowest levels of professional basketball. Somehow, Donny Walsh, the president of the Indiana Pacers, believed in what Larry could do. He would say that Bird had the ability to pull people together and that he was the epitome of the very fundamentals of basketball.[iv] That was why nobody in the Indiana Pacers organization had any problem with Larry Bird being named the head coach of the team in 1997. Bird's homecoming to Indiana was an immediate significant role with the state's NBA team.

Larry Bird was aware of his lack of experience in that field. He has spent all his life on the court playing basketball at the highest level possible. However, dozens of times it seemed like he was the extension of his coaches whether it was on the floor or the bench. On the court, Bird was technically the team's point guard because he was one of the primary playmakers. In team huddles, he was the leader that got his team pumped up. Those were the qualities that Walsh loved about him, and that was why everybody in the Pacers franchise had very high respects for Bird.

Bird had a lot of pressure on his shoulders coming into the 1997-98 season because he was essentially replacing a Hall of Fame coach in Larry Brown, but he would not let the difficulties of handling a team pull him down. What made life easy for him as well was that he was coaching mature veteran players in the likes of Reggie Miller, Mark Jackson, Rik Smits, and his former Olympic teammate, Chris Mullin. Bird injected new life into the Indiana team and they improved by as much as 19 wins from the previous season. Larry led the Pacers to a record of 58-24 and was named the NBA's Coach of the Year after only one season as the head honcho of the Indiana bench. He is the only man in the history of the NBA to win both the MVP and the Coach of the Year award. It was also during that year when Larry Bird was inducted and forever immortalized as a member of the Naismith Basketball Hall of Fame.

A veteran of many playoff games himself, Larry Bird would make the Pacers one of the most terrifying Eastern Conference squads. His team would cruise past the Cleveland Cavaliers in four games in the first round of the playoffs. In the second round, they would easily defeat the New York Knicks four games to one. With that series win against the Knicks, Larry Bird was back to the Conference Finals. This time, it was as a head coach. Bird would coach the Pacers in a hotly-contested

Conference Finals against the heavily-favored Chicago Bulls, who were the two-time defending champions.

Having played against Michael Jordan dozens of times when he was playing, Larry Bird knew how to shut down and defend the Greatest of All Time. If his boys could not do that, he at least knew how to make life difficult for Jordan. His experience as a player and his knowledge of the Bulls' superstars' tendencies were all too valuable in a dogfight for a chance to get to the NBA Finals.

After falling in the first two games, Bird got the Pacers back by winning two games in Indiana. It was in Game 4 when he drew up a play for Reggie Miller to get open and hit a game-winning three-pointer with less than a second left in the game. A Game 6 win forced a do-or-die final game. Despite a valiant effort from his guys, Bird and his Pacers were defeated in Game 7 of the Eastern Conference Finals.

Bird would come back the following year in a lockout-shortened NBA season. The teams would only play 50 games that season. Bird would coach his team to the second seed in the East with a record of 33-17. The Pacers were in full force coming into the postseason. They swept both the Milwaukee Bucks and the Philadelphia 76ers in the first and second rounds, respectively. But, somehow, they would lose to the underdog eighth-seeded New York Knicks in the Eastern Conference Finals.

The Hall of Famer would lead the Indiana Pacers to another strong year in the 1999-2000 season. It was going to be his final season as the head coach of the Pacers as he had previously promised to coach for only three seasons. He led his team to a record of 56-26 that season. The Pacers were in a good position yet again for a chance at the NBA championship since they were the first seed in the East coming into the postseason.

The Milwaukee Bucks, who were swept out of the playoffs by the Pacers a season ago, gave a good fight to Indiana. They would force Game 5, but would ultimately fall to the more experienced Pacer team. The Sixers, who also lost to the Pacers in the second round of the 1999 playoffs, would challenge Indiana well in the Eastern semis. After a valiant effort, Philadelphia would still lose in six games to the Pacers. Indiana would get revenge against the New York Knicks in the Eastern Conference Finals by beating them four games to two.

For the first time since 1987 when he was still a player, Larry Bird was back to the NBA Finals. In the Finals, the dominant Los Angeles Lakers were waiting. Coincidentally, the last time

Larry was in the Finals was against the Lakers led by his archrival Magic Johnson. This time, there was no Magic in LA. The Lakers were an entirely different team from the one that Bird used to have epic battles against in the 80's. In that season, the Laker team was led by the gigantic dominant center Shaquille O'Neal and the Jordan-esque young guard named Kobe Bryant. Against such a talented team, Bird's veteran squad was in for a tough battle for the NBA title.

In Game 1, all the talent that the Lakers had were too much for the Pacers to handle. Indiana would fall by 17 points. Despite a better effort in Game 2, Los Angeles would race to a 2-0 series lead over the Pacers. The Indiana Pacers would dig in deep into their veteran experience to win big time in Game 3. However, they would fall in a closely-fought Game 4 battle.

Down 1-3 and facing elimination, the Indiana Pacers would not quickly succumb to their might opponents. Bird coached a Pacers team that could not miss from the floor on their way to a 33-point win, which was the Lakers' worst Finals loss in franchise history. But when the series went back to Los Angeles for Game 6, the Lakers would once again deny Larry Bird of an NBA title after the franchise ended its 12-year championship drought.

Shortly after losing to the Los Angeles Lakers in the 2000 NBA Finals, Larry Bird stayed true to his word. He would resign as head coach after three successful seasons as the leader on the Pacer bench. Larry Bird took the Pacers to three consecutive Eastern Conference Finals and an NBA Finals appearance in his final season. His record as a head coach in three seasons was an impressive 147 wins against 67 losses. Larry's accomplishments as a head coach and his win-loss record in that regard further prove his reputation as a consummate winner.

## Executive Stint

Larry Bird would return to the Indiana Pacers in 2003. That time, it was not as a coach. He was named as the team's President of Basketball Operations. His primary roles were to control staff and coaching moves as well as drafting and free agency decisions.

Bird would have a stagnant career as an executive with the Pacers ever since Reggie Miller retired in the middle of the 2000's. But Larry would lead a Pacer comeback from behind the scenes as the decade ended. His notable draft choices were future All-Stars Danny Granger and Roy Hibbert. In the 2010 NBA Draft, he was the leading proponent of drafting future All-Star wingman Paul George. He also picked up capable guard

Lance Stephenson in the second round. During that season, his Pacers made a return to the NBA playoffs.

In the 2011-12 lockout-shortened season, the Indiana Pacers were a much-improved team. Bird hired Frank Vogel as the new permanent head coach of the Pacers after placing him on an interim basis in the previous season. Vogel instilled a defense-oriented mentality in the team as they clinched the third seed in the East with a record of 42-24. Bird's other main moves during that season were the acquisitions of George Hill and David West. Because of how he led a Pacers improvement that season, Larry Bird was named the NBA's Executive of the Year that season. With that, Bird became a major award winner in every role he took in the NBA whether it was as a player, a coach, or an executive. Indiana would reach as far as the second round that season.

During the offseason of 2012, Larry Bird announced that he would be stepping down as the Pacers' President of Basketball Operations. The reason for such was recurring health issues that troubled him during the grind of several long NBA seasons. A year later, he returned to that role after Pacers ownership assured to the public that Larry was back at full health.[xi]

# Chapter 6: Rivalry with Magic Johnson

Larry Bird forged a name for himself the moment he came into the league. He is singularly one of the best, if not the best, players of the 80's era. But there is no doubt that his stint in the NBA became even more colorful because of his rivalry with the Los Angeles Lakers' star point guard, Magic Johnson.

The two superstars and NBA greats started their long history even before they had memorable clashes in the professional league. Back then, Larry Bird was leading his Indiana State Sycamores to a historic season for the school. They were practically unbeatable on their way to the NCAA Finals. Meanwhile, Earvin Johnson was making his way to that stage by making magic with Michigan State. The young college stars met in a battle for the NCAA crown. After a good fight, it was Johnson and his team that came out with the title.

Their stories would not end there. As rookies, Larry and Magic were both key pieces in the revival of their respective franchises. Bird led the Celtics to one of the best single-season turnarounds in NBA history as they finished the year with a 61-21 record. On the flip side, Johnson joined a Laker team that already had Kareem Abdul-Jabbar to go up to a record of 60-22 in the 1979-80 regular season. Coincidentally, Larry and Magic both happened to play for the two most storied franchises and the two teams that had so many epic clashes in the past.

Larry Bird had the best performance as a first-year player that season, one in which he was named the Rookie of the Year over Magic Johnson. Bird would lead his team to the Eastern Conference Finals only to lose to Dr. J's Philadelphia 76ers. Meanwhile, Magic led his team all the way to the 1980 NBA Finals to beat the Sixers. He was named the Finals MVP after his performance as the starting center in Game 6.

Bird would come back the following season to win the 1981 NBA championship against the Houston Rockets. At that point, Larry and Magic were tied 1-1 as far as NBA titles. However, the rivalry had not yet blossomed despite a long history between the two teams. It was only noticed that both the Celtics and the Lakers were the two most watched and talked about teams in the NBA back then.

It was also during that time that tensions between the white and black populations began to resurface again. The Ronald Reagan administration focused on rolling back the benefits that unproductive welfare receivers were getting. Most of those families under the welfare programs were black. On the other hand, the white population welcomed the changes that the administration was instituting because they did not like the idea that the unproductive members of the community were simply leeching off of the taxes they were paying to the government.[vii]

The tensions between the white and black populations trickled down to sports. Of course, the two most popular teams at that time would play a representation of what was happening. In one corner, the Boston Celtics were a team that was predominantly composed of white players. It also did not help that the city of Boston was a hotbed for a large working class composed of white men. On the other end, the Lakers were dominated by African-American players. Los Angeles has always been known to be a city of mixed races.

Bird and Johnson also best represented their respective races and towns. Larry, while from Indiana, was as Boston as anybody could get. He was a hardworking blue collar man that did not love the flair and the spotlight as much as the next guy did. On the other hand, Magic had a personality and a smile as bright as the lights in downtown Los Angeles. His style of play also best represented the flashiness of Hollywood. They were simply two different players playing for two different teams representing two different classes. The rhetoric and differences only served to increase the rivalry between the two teams and between their respective fan bases.

The popularity and rivalry would only grow bigger when David Stern stepped into the shoes of the NBA commissioner. Stern's focus as the head honcho of the NBA was to drive in revenue through marketing and merchandising efforts. And of course, most of those efforts were focused on both the Celtics and the Lakers. What happened subsequently were the television and merchandise domination of both teams. You turned on the TV and you would see either the Celtics or the Lakers battling other teams, if not each other. You went to the store and you would mostly see Celtics and Lakers merchandise. With the growing popularity of the two teams, it was inevitable that they would meet for the most epic of clashes.

The clash would finally happen. Arguably the two best teams in their respective conferences, the Celtics and the Lakers met each other in the 1984 Finals for the first time in that decade and for the first time since Bird and Magic joined the NBA. After a hard-fought battle, Larry and his Celtics came out on top with Bird getting his second NBA championship and his first Finals MVP award. The two teams and the bitter archrivals would face again in another great Finals matchup at the end of the 1985 season. The LA Lakers would end up winning that bout as they evened the Finals head-to-head matchup 1-1.

Up until that point, everything between Larry Bird and Magic Johnson was all business, all about winning, and all about the NBA title. Their rivalry, outside all of the racial signifiers and the history surrounding the Celtics and the Lakers, was all about the competition. And that was all it was until 1986 when the two best players in the league met each other for a Converse sneaker commercial.

Larry Bird and Magic Johnson would have a chance to bond with each other when they were chosen to star in one of Converse's sneaker ads which was shot in Indiana. Johnson was hesitant at first because he did not want to go Bird's home in Indiana. After the first half of the shoot, Larry was kind enough to invite Magic into his home for lunch. From that point on, all rivalries went out the window. [xii]

The former enemies turned into friends when Larry Bird got to know who Earvin Johnson was, and vice versa. They were no longer representing white or black. They were no longer stars playing at the height of the Celtic-Laker rivalry. And they were no longer two different kinds of personalities. From then on, there was a mutual understanding that they were simply two excellent NBA players playing for the same goal, just as we are all humans trying to get by in this world. The former bitter rivals would become best friends.

The two superstars would meet once again in another NBA Finals in 1987. At that time, Larry Bird and his Celtics were hampered by a lot of injuries, but that did not stop them from putting on a good show. It was a close showdown in Game 4 of the Finals, and it was time for both stars to show up. With seconds remaining, Larry hit a clutch three-pointer to get the Celtics a two-point lead.

But it was Magic who would get the last laugh. Down by merely a point, Johnson drove the lane against Kevin McHale and went up for a running hook shot over the outstretched arms of the Celtic big man. The shot went in to give the Lakers the win and, ultimately, the championship in six games. Larry Bird and Magic Johnson would never meet again in the NBA Finals after that series.

Fast forward the rivalry to 1992 during the Olympic Games in Barcelona, Spain. However, there was no rivalry there because Bird and Johnson were teammates on the Dream Team. It was the only time the two transcendent talents got to play together. Bird would play his final organized basketball game when the Americans won the gold medal. After years of playing with injuries and after bearing the wear and tear of 13 fruitful and successful NBA seasons, Larry Bird would decide to retire from the NBA. In his retirement party in Boston, a familiar face showed up. Magic Johnson was there to cheer on and bid farewell to his rival and best friend. Earvin would go on to say that there would never be another Larry Bird.[xiii] He was right.

# Chapter 7: Larry Bird's Personal Life

Larry Bird was born in West Baden, Indiana, before the family moved to French Lick where he was raised and grew up. French Lick was a small town that had a little over a population of 2,000 people. He was born to parents Joe and Georgia Bird. Joe worked as a blue collar factory worker in French Lick to support his large family. Larry Bird was the fourth of six children. He grew up with five other siblings named Linda, Eddie, Jeff, Mike, and Mark.

Growing up with four other brothers helped Larry Bird's interest in numerous sports at a young age. Larry would play baseball, softball, and basketball together with his brothers when they were younger. It was only in high school when he settled on basketball.

When Larry Bird was in his senior year in high school, his parents Joe and Georgia would divorce. This led Georgia to try to support the family on her lonesome. A year later, Joe committed suicide. It was also during that time when Larry was in his first marriage with his wife Janet while trying to support their daughter Corrie. Larry and Janet would file for divorce after a short-lived marriage. Since then, Larry and Corrie would never have a good relationship as father and daughter, though the latter would say that she was happy for her dad's success.[xiv] Larry would remarry again in 1989. He and his new wife Dinah Mattingly have two adopted children named Conner and Mariah.

Larry Bird would form an epic rivalry with Magic Johnson in his NBA career. The Larry-Magic rivalry was the most popular one in professional sports at that era and is perhaps the greatest of its kind in the history of the NBA. Up until their meeting in the 1985 NBA Finals, Bird and Johnson were always bitter enemies. It all changed after they filmed a Converse commercial in 1986. From then on, Larry Bird and Magic Johnson forged a friendship that transcended beyond basketball.

# Chapter 8: Larry Bird's Impact on Basketball

There has never been a player in the history of the NBA like Larry Bird. Standing above 6'9", Larry had the size and length of a power forward. However, playing positions never described Bird's style on the court too well. He had the size of a power forward, but he moved with the grace of a guard. His training as a shooting guard in high school helped him develop the deadliest shooting stroke in all of basketball during the 80's era. Combined with his length and size, he was un-guardable when he decided to go up for a jump shot. That was why despite his lack of athleticism and dominating strength, Larry Bird was able to put up points up on the board in bunches even as he aged into his 30's.

But his offense was not the only skill that made Larry Bird the best player of his time. At his size, Bird could rebound at a rate similar to centers and other big men. For the first six seasons of his career, he averaged double digits in rebounding. Aside from that, Bird was one of the most gifted passers the NBA has seen at the small forward spot. With his length, he could see over the defenses and make plays for his teammates in the half court set.

And when he got rebounds, he was one of the best outlet passers that could get the ball to streaking players.

Defensively, Bird was never a slacker. He did not have the foot speed to keep up with athletic and quick players, but he defended well by anticipating their movements. Instead of trying to keep up with every step, he would beat his opponents to the position. Bird's court vision and his great anticipation skills also got him dozens of steals. Nobody could ever forget when Bird intercepted an Isiah Thomas inbound pass during the 1987 East Finals. That steal got the Celtics the lead and a Finals appearance.

With all those skills combined, one could understand why Magic Johnson said that the world would never see another player like Larry Bird. Bird had the size of a power forward, the touch of a shooting guard, the passing skills and court vision of a point guard, and the rebounding abilities of a center. He did all that despite lacking the natural speed and athleticism of his African-American counterparts.

Though no player in the history of the NBA up until now has developed into the type of player Larry Bird was in his prime years, there have been a few who have come close. First came Kevin Garnett in 1995. Garnett at about 7 feet tall made his living in the NBA by shooting jump shots from the perimeter. He was also a very gifted rebounder and a terrific passer at the power forward position.

Then there was German 7-footer Dirk Nowitzki. Dirk was a trained shooter back when he was still in Germany, and when he came to the NBA, he' made good use of his shooting skills and length to create perimeter mismatches and shoot over the top of smaller defenders much like Larry Bird used to do. The Boston Celtics even attempted to relive Bird's memories by going after Nowitzki in the 1998 NBA Draft. However, the Dallas Mavericks beat them to the punch.

Though he is not a shooter of Bird's caliber, LeBron James is every bit of an all-around player that Larry was. Putting his otherworldly athleticism aside, LeBron came into the league as a complete player that could do anything on the floor. He could score, rebound, and defend all at very high levels. But it was his passing skills that always impressed people most. Like Bird, James was a big man that could see the floor well and make plays for other people by using crisp and precise passes. Had he been a great shooter, he could have very well been the next coming of Larry Bird.

Another player similar to Larry Bird is Kevin Durant. At about 6'10", Kevin Durant came into the NBA as a matchup nightmare at the small forward position. He was a lot quicker than most of his counterparts and was bigger than the few guys that could keep up with him. With his size and length, Durant shot over his defenders with ease on his way to four scoring championships and an MVP award in the NBA. While not the playmaker or the defender that Bird was, Durant was always capable in those aspects of the game on top of his good rebounding abilities.

With those players in mind, you can never put into words how much Larry Bird changed and impacted the game of basketball. He was one of the few players that transcended size and playing positions. He was a big man that could play every kind of position on the floor while doing everything else at high levels. But the one thing you can never discount from Larry was how hard he competed and how hard he did his best to win games and championships. It is no wonder why most of the players he has impacted or that have patterned their games after him have become MVP's and champions. After all, being a winner was always Bird's lasting impact as a basketball player.

# Chapter 9: Larry Bird's Legacy

No matter from what angle you look at his career, or from whatever generation's point of view you use, Larry Bird is and will always be one of the greatest NBA players the world has ever seen. Not convinced? Look at his numbers. He has amassed a total of 21,791 career points, 8,974 career rebounds, 5,695 career assists, and 1,556 career steals in only 12 seasons in the NBA. But numbers pale in comparison to what he has achieved as a player and a winner. He was the 1980 Rookie of the Year, the third out of only three players to win the MVP award for three consecutive seasons, and was an NBA champion three times.

If you are not yet convinced that Bird is one of the greatest of all time, look at what he meant to the Boston Celtics franchise and to the NBA during the 80's era. Bird came to the Boston Celtics in 1979 and immediately turned the team around from only winning 29 games a season before, to championship contenders. For three consecutive years under his leadership, the Celtics won at least 60 games. In his 12 full seasons in the franchise, the team had six seasons of 60 or more wins. The other six seasons were at least 50-win years for the Boston

Celtics. The only time the Celtics could not win above 50 was when Bird was out for the majority of the season in 1988-89.

Those facts and his numbers as a player would also put Larry Bird on top of all the players that have played for the Boston Celtics franchise. That is not an easy feat to put on Bird considering that legendary names such as Bob Cousy, Bill Russell, Sam Jones, John Havlicek, Dave Cowens, Kevin McHale, and Paul Pierce have all contributed significantly to the franchise in their respective generations. Though the Celtics have had the luxury of being able to field those great players in their long history, Larry bird is arguably the franchise's best player ever.

It may be true that Bird does not have the 11 championship rings that Bill Russell has. He does not even come close to the number of titles that both Jones and Havlicek have. He is not even second to Hondo's career points with the Celtics. But Bird's ability to transcend generations and his all-around skills put him together with, if not just above those names.

Larry Bird singlehandedly transformed and won titles for the Boston Celtics while garnering personal awards for himself as soon as he donned the green uniform. He was even doing it in arguably the toughest era of NBA basketball as compared to when Russell, Jones, and Havlicek were winning titles, back when the NBA was a very modest league and was not as competitive as it is now.

Throughout the 80's, Larry Bird had to play against a prime Julies Erving's Sixers team in his early days. He played against the MVP form of Moses Malone for his first NBA championship, with the likes of Dominique Wilkins, Isiah and his Bad Boys, Karl Malone and John Stockton, a rising Charles Barkley, and a young Michael Jordan in his athletic prime among others. He even had to compete against the Showtime Los Angeles Lakers of Magic Johnson when that franchise was in its best era.

Despite the stiff competition that Larry Bird and his Boston Celtics had to face in that period concerning superstar player and team quality, he still came out with three MVP awards and three championship rings. Along the way, he even changed the landscape of the NBA and the way it is being played right now while maintaining to stay competitive and elite as he aged.

Larry Bird was not only changing the Boston Celtic franchise but also the whole NBA landscape as well. Before his arrival, the league was struggling to get viewership, television deals, a fan base, and merchandise sales back in the 70's. Bird's landing in the NBA could not have come at a better time. His phenomenal rise to the top of the league brought excitement to fans of both the Celtics and the NBA. He embodied what it meant to work hard and compete, and that blue collar mentality made him even more famous as he led his team to playoff wins and championships.

Larry Bird could have reached the heights of his popularity and his fame by his lonesome. He was leading his team to championships, and he was winning MVP's by playing his all-around style of hard-nosed basketball. But what got him the reputation of a pop culture icon was his rivalry with Magic Johnson and his team's battles with the Los Angeles Lakers.

Both Bird and Johnson came into the league in the same season. And, at the same time, the two superstars brought their respective teams back to the top of the NBA food chain by playing the role of the all-around star to perfection. As the Celtics and the Lakers both rose to the top of their respective conferences, it was inevitable for them to ultimately meet for the top prize of the NBA.

The two best players leading the two best teams would meet for the NBA championship for the first time in the 1984 Finals. That was when the rivalry between Larry Bird and Magic

Johnson blossomed into the legend it is to this date. Bird and Johnson battled it out for supremacy that season, but it was the Celtics that came out with the NBA trophy in 1984.

Seeing as how viewership and ratings went through the roof when either or both the Celtics and the Lakers were on television, then-NBA commissioner David Stern focused the league's marketing strategies around Larry and Magic. Their popularity and rivalry only grew bigger. They would meet once again in the 1985 Finals for a rematch of 1984's championship bout. Magic would tie their head-to-head Finals record by going home with the 1985 trophy.

The rubber match was fought in 1987. In what would become their last meeting in the NBA Finals, Larry Bird and Magic Johnson, who were already great friends at that time, battled it out in a tough series to determine the 1987 champions. Johnson and his Lakers came out on top of that one to win the head-to-head Finals matchup with Larry Bird.

Because of Bird's decade-long rivalry with Johnson, the NBA was even more exciting to watch during the 1980's era. That popularity paved the way for the NBA to become what it is right now—arguably the most-watched professional sports league in the world.

Because of what Larry Bird has accomplished as a player, as a winner, and as a cultural icon, one can understand why he is consistently considered to be one of the top players the league has ever seen and why he is considered as a player that transcended generations. You look at his numbers, his awards, his championships, and the myriad of players he has inspired to pick up a basketball and work hard to become great. By simply doing that, you would see how valuable Larry Bird truly has been to the NBA, even now as he leads the Indiana Pacers front office. It is only fitting to reiterate what Magic Johnson said about him. There will never be another Larry Bird.

# Final Word/About the Author

I was born and raised in Norwalk, Connecticut. Growing up, I could often be found spending many nights watching basketball, soccer, and football matches with my father in the family living room. I love sports and everything that sports can embody. I believe that sports are one of most genuine forms of competition, heart, and determination. I write my works to learn more about influential athletes in the hopes that from my writing, you the reader can walk away inspired to put in an equal if not greater amount of hard work and perseverance to pursue your goals. If you enjoyed *Larry Bird: The Inspiring Story of One of Basketball's Greatest Forwards*, please leave a review! Also, you can read more of my works on *Calvin Johnson, Colin Kaepernick, Aaron Rodgers, Peyton Manning, Tom Brady, Russell Wilson, Michael Jordan, LeBron James, Kyrie Irving, Klay Thompson, Stephen Curry, Kevin Durant, Russell Westbrook, Anthony Davis, Chris Paul, Blake Griffin, Kobe Bryant, Joakim Noah, Scottie Pippen, Carmelo Anthony, Kevin Love, Grant Hill, Tracy McGrady, Vince Carter, Patrick Ewing, Karl Malone, Tony Parker, Allen Iverson, Hakeem Olajuwon, Reggie Miller, Michael Carter-Williams, John Wall, James Harden, Tim Duncan, Steve Nash, Pau Gasol, Marc Gasol, Jimmy Butler, Dirk Nowitzki, Draymond Green, Pete Maravich,*

*Kawhi Leonard, Dwyane Wade, Ray Allen, Paul George, Paul Pierce, and Manu Ginobili* in the Kindle Store. If you love basketball, check out my website at [claytongeoffreys.com](claytongeoffreys.com) to join my exclusive list where I let you know about my latest books and give you lots of goodies.

# Like what you read? Please leave a review!

I write because I love sharing the stories of influential people like Larry Bird with fantastic readers like you. My readers inspire me to write more so please do not hesitate to let me know what you thought by leaving a review! If you love books on life, basketball, or productivity, check out my website at claytongeoffreys.com to join my exclusive list where I let you know about my latest books. Aside from being the first to hear about my latest releases, you can also download a free copy of *33 Life Lessons: Success Principles, Career Advice & Habits of Successful People*. See you there!

*Clayton*

# References

[i] Marcovici, Alon. "A Decade of Parity". *NBA Encyclopedia*. Web

[ii] Merlino, Doug. "Magic Johnson and Larry Bird: The Rivalry That Transformed the NBA". *Bleacher Report*. 13 May 2011. Web

[iii] "Larry Bird". *Notable Biographies*. Web

[iv] "Larry Bird". *NBA Encyclopedia*. Web

[v] Extra Mustard. "Check Out a Scouting Report on Larry Bird from 1984". *Sports Illustrated*. 26 January 2015. Web

[vi] Schwartz, Larry. "Plain and Simple, Bird one of the Best". *ESPN*. Web

[vii] Merlino, Doug. "Magic Johnson and Larry Bird: The Rivalry That Transformed the NBA". *Bleacher Report*. 13 May 2011. Web

[viii] "10 Fascinating Facts About Larry Bird". *Buzz Reaper*. 25 December 2015. Web

[ix] Fromal, Adam. "Larry Bird's 25 Greatest Career Moments to Honor Larry Legend's 57th Birthday". *Bleacher Report*. 6 December 2013. Web

[x] "1992 United States Olympic Team". *Naismith Memorial Basketball Hall of Fame.*

[xi] "Bird Returns". *NBA.com*. 26 June 2013. Web

[xii] "Larry Bird and Magic Johnson Reveal the 1986 Sneaker Commercial That Took Them From Bitter Rivals to Best Friends". *Daily Mail UK*. 12 April 2012. Web

[xiii] "Classic NBA Quotes: Magic and Larry". *NBA Encyclopedia*. Web

[xiv] Hughes, David. "Longing for a Lasting Bond". *Tribune Star*. Web

Made in the USA
Middletown, DE
24 March 2020

87185069R00068